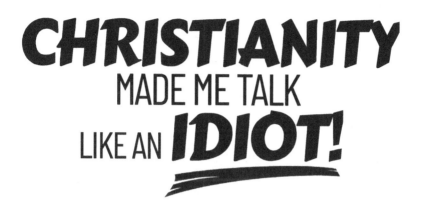

CHRISTIANITY
MADE ME TALK
LIKE AN *IDIOT!*

D1446882

SETH ANDREWS

outskirts
press

This book is available in audiobook format at **Audible.com**, *read by the author.*

Table of Contents

Foreword i

Introduction v

Chapter One: If Humans Came from Monkeys –
The Ironies of Evolution Denial 1

Chapter Two: The Devil Has Your Number –
Paranoia and Panic from the Divinely Protected 15

Chapter Three: Strange Passion –
Easter Torture Theater 33

Chapter Four: Eat Jesus –
The Creepy, Culty Ritual of Communion 45

Chapter Five: Look to the East –
Thoughts on the Second Coming of Christ 55

Chapter Six: Hell If I Know –
When Christians Don't Know Their Bibles 63

Chapter Seven: Explain It to Me –
The Calamity of Christian Apologetics 75

Chapter Eight: Bob's Bicycle –
Prayer, Priorities, and the God of Diminishing Returns 87

Chapter Nine: Jesus Is Rated G –
   Puritan America's War on the Naked Body 105

Chapter Ten: Teens and Designer Jeans –
   The Blaming and Shaming of Purity Culture........................ 121

Chapter Eleven: Come Lord Jesus –
   Anxieties of the Earthbound Believer 139

Chapter Twelve: The Hands of the Surgeon –
   Healing, Hypocrisy, and the Church 147

Chapter Thirteen: Christianese –
   A Religion in Bumper Stickers... 161

Chapter Fourteen: Cherry Picking –
   The Custom-Fitting of Cafeteria Christianity 177

Chapter Fifteen: Reflection –
   Pointing the Finger Back at Myself 187

Acknowledgments 191

Endnotes.. 192

Foreword

The ability to laugh at oneself is underrated. If we can chuckle about the hairstyles we had, the clothes we wore, and even the music we listened to, we can have both an understanding of who we were and an appreciation for who we have become.

Without that skill, we are stuck. We may have progressed, but if we can't look back with fondness and understanding, we can't fully know and love ourselves. There is something revelatory and therapeutic about remembering the thoughts and emotions we were experiencing at a particular point in time, and, gently laughing, forgive and accept who and where we were.

Seth Andrews has found, honed, and sharpened that skill. With utter compassion for himself and others on similar journeys, he has created this opportunity for us to peek through a window into the past.

As he himself says, he wasn't an idiot, and he doesn't think others are idiots, for having said some idiotic things. With his signature sharp wit and charming personality, he describes the frog-in-boiling-water situation in which so many of us found ourselves when we began to open the door to questioning and doubting our beliefs.

Then, ever so logically, he examines the words, concepts, and phrases that guided our lives and that we could say in our sleep. He unpacks their head-scratching, and sometimes jaw-dropping, meanings in the light of reason and rationality.

"Everything happens for a reason."

Everything? Really? Guinea worms burrowing out the eyeball of a five-year-old?

"Ask and ye shall receive."

How many of us fervently, authentically, and consistently embraced this concept, asking and begging and pleading for help in an unbearable situation, and received the hollow, echoing emptiness of silence?

"God's way are higher than our ways."

In what universe, and under what circumstances, is it remotely moral to "dash the little ones against the rocks" (Psalm 137:9) and "take the younger women as your own" (1 Tim. 5:2)?

Wait, what?

After the shock dissipates and we truly examine a deeply held belief, we blink, sigh, and look around to see if anyone else saw our foolishness.

But Seth doesn't leave us shaking our heads in red-faced embarrassment. He encourages us to look again, go deeper, to thoroughly question *all* of the premises upon which we built lives, community, and relationships. He shows us the value of skepticism applied earnestly and honestly. He guides us toward examining the next belief, and the next, and the next.

This book may seem to be a series of lighthearted, anecdotal stories that poke fun at silly supernatural beliefs. This may be true for readers who have never fervently held those beliefs. But for a great many of us, the dismantling of those beliefs may be seismic. While the book cover may look like the entrance to an amusement park, the reader's journey through the chapters may be as serious and life-changing as any college philosophy course, pivotal emotional experience, or profound personal realization.

Reading this book will not fail to bring a smile. Whether you are confident in your spiritual journey, just dipping your big toe into the vast ocean of doubt, or have rejected religion outright, you will enjoy this delightful romp into the complicated and connected world of language, faith, and logic.

Don your helmet of skepticism and breastplate of reason. You're going to love the ride.

Gayle Jordan, Executive Director, Recovering from Religion

Introduction

I wrestled with the title of this book. I knew that it would get people talking, yet attention needs to be drawn for the right reasons. The topics I address here speak to claims, ideas, and beliefs, but we are talking about beliefs linked directly to identity, so when I challenge religious thoughts and behaviors, the devout might feel like I am stabbing them in the heart. This is the dilemma. How do I challenge nonsense without offending those who believe in nonsense?

Obviously, I kept the title. It's self-deferential. It's catchy. And I think Christians deserve better than to be patted on the head with an attitude of diminished expectations. "Oh, I don't want to hurt feelings" is partially the reason we are surrounded by unreason, and frankly, any God worth his or her salt would be unperturbed by my humble scribblings here. If omnipotent Yahweh can't be harmed by it, believers shouldn't be alarmed by it.

I was also influenced by religious doubters who stumbled upon my 2017 YouTube speech by the same title and emailed their various thank yous. One man named Jason wrote, "You said out loud what I've been feeling inside for years. I always had a problem with the Bible but never knew how to articulate my feelings." For Jason and those like him, "Christianity Made Me Talk Like an Idiot" validated concerns and doubts bubbling just under their skin. Many were carrying the heavy mantle of an inherited religion passed down from family and culture, and when they tired of shouldering the burden because "that's what Christians do," they began committing the near-unpardonable sin: they raised the hand of challenge. They asked sensible questions: Is the Bible true? Are the scriptures accurate and moral? Are my faith traditions logical and helpful? Was I ever given a choice? And perhaps most importantly, Have I done my own thinking?

Tragically, many pay a significant personal price for the crime of independent thought. Christ ordered lockstep allegiance: "If you love me, keep my commands."[1] Doubters in the Bible were not treated kindly (see Thomas the Apostle), and the same is often true for doubters today. Fundamentalism is a culture of what the philosopher Daniel Dennett calls "belief in belief," and any diversion from the straight and narrow can bring serious consequences: Loss of trust. Loss of a job. Loss of family, friends, and community. All the while, Christianity sells the circular conclusion that "it's true because we believe it, and we believe it because it's true." The faithful engage with often bizarre convictions and rituals, defiantly proclaiming that no question, concern, objection, refutation, or fact will ever cause them to change their minds.

The point is that religion often acts like the Ceti eels from *Star Trek II: The Wrath of Khan*, turning the otherwise reasonable brain into a blindly compliant obedience machine. Evangelical Christians, primed from their formative years, receive instructions from authority and simply carry out their orders. Reason becomes an enemy, a doorway for the Devil. Evangelist Joyce Meyer echoed this warning as she instructed child-rearing parents: "Satan will look for your child's weakest area and attack at that point. He will attempt to fill your child with worry, reasoning, fear, depression, and discouraging negative thoughts."[2]

Yes, Meyer aligned reason with worry, fear, depression, negativity, and even Satan himself. Critical thinking is a problem. Deference, belief, and obedience are the way. In this, we again see the dilemma. I would wager that Joyce Meyer doesn't take this approach in other aspects of her life. She has almost certainly challenged authority, or argued with a philosophical point, or criticized and dismantled a competing faith. Yet her own sacred doctrine remains a foreigner to reasoning (or at least a victim of bad reasoning), leading her—and a host of her fellow believers—to speak and act in strange and ridiculous ways.

Is Joyce Meyer an idiot? I don't think so, but she often sounds like one. When I was a devout Christian, I was much the same. I am not saying that Christians are idiots. At least, they aren't idiots any more than the average person.

My examples don't address the exceptions. The best I can do is to acknowledge here that exceptions exist, that the wide, wild spectrum of Christian faith is practiced in varying ways, and that those who don't fit into my descriptions deserve credit for carving their own unique paths. Religions are often reflections of the complex people who hold them. They are cherry-picked and molded and personalized like a Spotify playlist, but the unreasonable teachings and trends still exist, and those are fair game.

This book is my attempt to reverse-engineer some of my own non-sensical behaviors and expand that lens to examine mainstream Christianity in the United States. I want to explore ostensibly sensible Christianity. I want to understand how our evolved brains can generate regressive notions. And I want to challenge believers to take another look at the "normal" attitudes and activities that, to many of the rest of us, seem like lunacy. The believer may well not be an idiot, but very often, he or she certainly sounds like one.

CHAPTER ONE

If Humans Came from Monkeys – The Ironies of Evolution Denial

On March 22, 1871, the satirical magazine *The Hornet* published a caricature illustration of the famous English naturalist and biologist Charles Darwin, author of the groundbreaking book *On the Origin of Species*. In the illustration, Darwin is drawn as hunched over, with an exaggerated jawline and the hairy body of an ape.

This image reflects how millions of American evangelicals continue to feel about Darwin's theory of evolution. Evolution is a cartoon. A joke. Ridiculous. A 2018 Pew Research survey revealed that 38 percent of white evangelical Protestants still insist that humans have always existed in their current form: created, not evolved.[3] That is

"A Venerable Orang-outang". The Hornet 3-22-1871

more than *one in three* Americans. As bioethicist and author Melanie Challenger notes, "The world is now dominated by an animal that doesn't think it is an animal, and the future is being imagined by an animal that doesn't want to be an animal."[4] This denial of reality is nowhere more prevalent than in the minds of the Bible literalists.

Strangely, the my-granddaddy-wasn't-no-monkey creationists eagerly embrace the biblical claim that they are the descendants of a dirt-man and rib-woman who were conjured into an enchanted garden by an all-powerful wizard with a hang-up about trees and talking snakes. It is the twenty-first century, yet this is where we are. The proven primate is a punchline; the magical man is legitimate. Why? Because "the Bible tells me so."

Creationists ask ridiculous questions, such as, "If humans came from monkeys, why are there still monkeys?" The premise of the question is already problematic: humans and monkeys have a common ancestor; humans didn't "come from" monkeys. It is the equivalent of asking, If the biblical Adam came from the dirt, why is there still dirt? If Americans came from Britain, why is there still a Britain? If the Missouri River flows into the Mississippi River, why is there still a Missouri River? You get the idea.

In my evangelical years, I was irony incarnate: a primate mocking primates. All the while, I was a walking, talking billboard for my evolutionary ancestors. My body has hair on the arms, legs, and chest, a useless evolutionary leftover from the times when my hairy animal relatives insulated themselves against cold weather.[5] The goose bumps that raise the hair on my arms and neck once kept my primate ancestors warmer in cold weather and made them appear larger and more formidable against threats.[6] The swelling around my wisdom teeth betrays the larger jaws of my hunter-gatherer ancestors.[7] (I find it ironic that 85 percent of "intelligently designed" adults in the United States have their wisdom teeth extracted to prevent pain, infection, and damage to other teeth.[8]) In my sixth week in the womb, I temporarily had an embryonic tail known as a coccyx—a remnant from primate forebears who used tails for balance and movement within the trees.[9] (Interestingly, in rare cases, babies are born with those tails still intact.) Those weird little pink indentions at the insides of my eyes—the *plica semilunaris*—are residuals from animal relatives who blinked horizontally instead of vertically.[10] Even my pubic hair harkens back to the reproductive signaling of my ancestral past, once functioning as pheromone broadcasters of sexual maturity and availability.[11]

As a devout Christian, I felt insulted that anyone might associate me with those hairy, grunting, tree-swinging, knuckle-dragging animals. I wasn't an animal. I was above the animals, beyond the animals, given dominion over the animals:

> Then God said, "Let us make humankind in our image, according to our likeness; and let them have dominion over the fish of the sea, and over the birds of the air, and over the cattle, and over all the wild animals of the Earth, and over every creeping thing that creeps upon the Earth."[12]

This Bible verse is reminiscent of the philosophy of Rene Descartes, who wrote in 1637 that "animals are mere machines, but man stands alone."[13] Descartes saw animals as instinctive, reactive creatures without a soul.[14] In his view, animals barked and squawked and mimicked in a primitive world, beyond thoughtfulness, beyond language, beyond the transcendent plane of human existence. Animals couldn't effectively process distinctly human feelings and expressions, such as love or angst. They flung about in the muck, lesser beings living under our dominion, for our uses, and by our pleasure.

This human superiority complex remains widely prevalent, even among those with a more charitable view of animal souls, and any ranking would still list the human soul as most important.

As a creationist and Bible literalist, I couldn't imagine a soul residing inside a gorilla. Or a parrot. Or a whale, racoon, or anaconda. I remember one tragic Sunday church sermon during which the preacher informed his congregation—including their horrified children—that dogs cannot go to Heaven. Of course, a Heaven without dogs sounds like a cheerless gulag, but the claim lines up with the doctrine that the soul is the lone domain of the human non-animal.

I think that doctrine serves several purposes. First, a disconnect from other life forms makes it easier to place humans in a Members Only club. From the high mountain, we can glare down our noses at the lesser creatures, content to use (and even abuse) them with the excuse from Genesis that they exist to serve us. In the planetary hierarchy, humans are divinely placed at the very top, and the rest of the planet will just have to deal with dominion.

The idea of divine specialness serves the ego. Ancient astronomers believed that Earth was the literal center of the universe (geocentrism). This notion so infected fundamentalist Bible believers that when the astronomer Galileo used new telescope technology to reveal the blasphemous fact that the sun didn't revolve around the Earth, he was placed on trial as a heretic by the Roman Catholic Inquisition and locked away on home confinement for the rest of his life. For humans to *not* be the center of all things was unthinkable, as that claim might indicate a vast, uncaring universe, where life was finite and personal destinies might not be handed down from on high. What a terrifying challenge to the conceits of created man.

In the game of life, the We're Number One! cheerleading keeps people from looking at the scoreboard. In other words, declaring and defending a truth is much easier than validating one. Reading one book (the Bible?) is simpler than digging through the mountains of evidentiary scientific texts and their often inconvenient findings. Humans gravitate toward simple solutions, cut-and-dry binary models that easily fit into our mental molds. When things get messy or overly complicated, we blink ourselves back toward the quick, the safe, and the familiar. The biblical creation story requires just a few verses. The highly complex story of human evolution and our place in the universe span whole libraries.

Regarding hot-button issues such as evolutionary science, changing minds by using data is uncommon. For those with strongly held convictions, contradicting evidence causes intense discomfort, called cognitive dissonance; their brains immediately bend backward to realign and reshape the world in a way that restores mental harmony.[15] The activated amygdala triggers a defensive mode against all perceived attacks upon the self, often producing a backfire effect that further entrenches original opinions.[16] Present the hard evidence for evolution, and the believer might go rigid and defensive, protesting, "I'm not a monkey! I'm a child of God! I'll never change my mind on this!"

Do you ever wonder why verbal exchanges get so passionate and contentious when they involve firmly held religious or political beliefs? Those beliefs are linked to values, identity, and the self. Feeling targeted, the brain short-circuits, the fight-or-flight reflex kicks into overdrive, and we treat an ideological threat just as we would a physical threat.[17] We aren't climbing up walls to get a better viewpoint; we are frantically reinforcing our walls from within because we feel unsafe. This happens frequently in debates, and it certainly happens in clashes between creationists and the proponents of evolutionary science.

It is true that when looked at from a distance, evolution doesn't appear intuitive. There are humans, and there are animals. But what are animals?

By definition, animals are multicellular organisms. They are *heterotrophic*, meaning that, unlike plants, which produce their own nutrients, animals can't get their nutrition from inorganic sources such as sunlight, but instead must depend on other organisms for food. Animals generally have the capacity to move at will. They have specialized sensory organs (eyes, ears, skin, etc.) that respond to the surrounding environment. They reproduce sexually. They breathe in oxygen and exhale carbon dioxide. Most animals possess a lymphatic system, muscular system, nervous system, reproductive system, respiratory system, skeletal system, and urinary system. Most animals are bilaterally symmetric (left and right eyes, arms, legs, etc.), and they experience four fundamental life cycle stages: infancy, youth, adulthood, and senescence. Sound familiar?

The human animal is, in fact, a primate; our DNA is 99 percent identical to chimpanzees and bonobos and 98 percent identical to gorillas.[18] Primates have a similar body shape, like mannerisms, fingered hands and toed feet, and similar skulls that contain large brains.

Many ostensibly human qualities can easily be seen throughout the animal kingdom, especially in primates. In an article for the Jane Goodall Institute of Canada, journalist Anna Muir posted video clips showing chimpanzees laughing when tickled, recognizing themselves in mirrors, using tools to procure food, and organizing and hunting in groups. Chimps often "kiss, hug, pat each other on the back, shake their fists," throw tantrums, enjoy close-knit social groups, and "demonstrate a range of emotions including joy, sadness, fear, and even empathy."[19]

The famous Dutch-American primatologist Frans de Waal wrote *Mama's Last Hug: Animal Emotions and What They Tell Us about Ourselves*, which delves deeply into the emotional bonds, thoughtful behaviors, family units, and moral reasoning evident in non-human primates. He notes that the apes we caricaturize as unwashed brutes do, in fact, socialize with each other, protect each other, provide for each other, find joy with each other, and grieve the loss of others in their group. Ignoring this reality risks ignoring critical links between humans and the rest of our evolved natural world. A former Catholic, de Waal says, "The more I think about it, the more I think it is a very dangerous position that we have taken in the west—that religions have fostered—that we are a special creation and that we don't have the same connections with nature as everyone else."[20]

It is tragic. As the creationist dominionist huffs and condescends to lesser beings, his beloved myths and magic leave no room for the real magic of the natural world. It is true that some denominations of Christianity have, ironically, evolved away from a literal interpretation of Genesis, editing their doctrines to allow for a "guided evolution," but they continue to protect the Adam-Eve story as allegory. This allows them to clumsily insist that the Genesis fruit fable bears some transcendent truth about the holiness of God and the sinful human heart.

As an atheist, I have re-read the creation account dozens of times, and I can't imagine what an original sin allegory could possibly mean. Adam and Eve weren't the first humans, or the only humans, but they represent humanity in some way? If there wasn't a literal Garden of Eden, what would a garden symbolize? What could the Tree of the Knowledge of Good and Evil teach us, especially against the claim that God placed the tree in plain view of vulnerable children, making him even more the tempter than the villainous talking serpent?

How does human nakedness fit into the allegory, and what relation does disobedience have to fig leaves covering the penis, vagina, and female breasts? How could the story of casting off Adam and Eve (and their billions of descendants) over a harmless mistake demonstrate unconditional love? What does Eve's punishment of painful child-bearing imply? Or life beyond the garden? Or a serpent cursed to slither on the ground? And doesn't the whole Shakespearean tragedy reveal a tremendous lack of aptitude and foresight by a god that is supposed to be the smartest, wisest, and most all-knowing being in the history of everything?

Ask a devout believer about these things, and you will likely get a bumper sticker: Man Failed. God Is Good. Free Will. These same creation-as-metaphor Christians will likely still insist that all life is intelligently designed, a creationism-lite position that allows them to slot their Bibles on the bookshelf right next to Charles Darwin, Thomas Huxley, and Stephen J. Gould. The best of both worlds.

A great example of this (dare I say it) *adaptation* is the Roman Catholic Church, which didn't jump onto the evolutionary bandwagon until the mid-twentieth century. That is two thousand years of selling the "creation truth" before switching gears to sell the "evolution truth" after the scientific evidence became impossible to ignore. Many mainstream Christian churches have similarly adapted a little Darwin into their doctrines to stay relevant. "Oh. Yeah. Well, sure we evolved. But who set evolution into motion? *Our God!*"

I have yet to meet any evangelical Christians who don't still wince at a kinship with apes, their divine specialness safe and secure. Some lean in to the abiogenesis argument: as we don't yet know how the first cells of life originated, the implication is that they were created, and that creation proves the creator. The first cell propelled complex life, which was always intended.

Christian apologists love to talk about complexity, yet I have become convinced that they are conflating complexity with design. They gape, overwhelmed, at wildly complicated or confusing mechanisms, still convinced that humans are an end result of a brilliant engineer's plan. Of course, the best designs are optimized into their simplest and most efficient forms, raising legitimate questions about the baggage of genetic redundancies, junk DNA, physical inefficiencies, and so on. And even if a designer autographed his handiwork with a "signature in the cell" (the title of a 2009 book by religious scientist Dr. Stephen Meyer), the implication is that God hid the proof of his involvement from the billions who lived before humans invented the microscope.

How intelligent is this design, anyway? Even a cursory glance reveals a planet that seems quite uninterested in human progress or safety. Every day people get swallowed up in sinkholes, pummeled by hailstorms, swept into hurricanes and tornadoes, buried by earthquakes, drowned by tsunamis, and slapped around by the uncaring mechanisms of nature. Seventy-one percent of the planet is liquid and unlivable for humans, and 97 percent of Earth's water is undrinkable.

Our sunlight gives us skin cancer. Blind animals, like the Brazilian characid, have useless eyes. Ostriches have large wings, yet the highest they can get airborne is when they jump a three-foot fence. Whales have no legs, yet they still have pelvises for legs, and despite being ocean-bound creatures, they are forced to constantly surface for air so they do not drown. Giraffes have a laryngeal nerve that detours an extra fourteen feet before it gets to its connection point, wrapping down the long neck and around the heart in an unnecessary loop. The list of weird, bad design goes on and on, and humans aren't exempt.

Zoologist Abby Hafer wrote the book *The Not-So-Intelligent*

Designer,[21] which reveals how ridiculous much of our human "design" looks beyond the lens of evolution. Why would a designer place the reproductively critical and tremendously sensitive male testicles in an exposed and easily kickable skin bag, especially seeing as how other creatures have their reproductive organs hidden safely within the body? And why would he make testicles so susceptible to pain in the first place? (Thanks, God.) Why do human females have a birth canal that painfully stretches cartilage and ligaments, separates pelvic bones, and rips skin? What kind of design naturally aborts roughly half of all pregnancies before they come to term? Why place the human windpipe adjacent to the esophagus, resulting in hundreds of choking deaths every year? Why does the human eye have an optic nerve that goes through the surface of the retina, creating a blind spot and requiring the brain to compensate? Why do animal teeth, including those in the human animal, trap bacteria that then lead to tooth and gum infections? Dr. Hafer's book is a must-read on questions like these.

Of course, creationists (I lump them in with the intelligent design crowd) have an easy out when challenged about this stuff: the sin of humankind. Yes, God once set into motion a perfect design, but after that unfortunate first incident in the garden, an evil wrench was tossed into the machine. Genomic DNA became unnecessarily cluttered with useless code and predispositions for diseases. Hemlock and nightshade became poisonous and deadly. Previously vegan lions, crocodiles, and sharks started chewing on live animal flesh. Benign sunbeams developed dangerous UV radiation. Children became hosts for leukemia, their fathers collapsed with blood clots, their birth mothers screamed in the delivery rooms. God's best-laid plan totally went to shit—and it is all our fault.

This is one of the more insidious shades of the intelligent design position because even those pitching a more nebulous, faceless designer still often insinuate that humanity screwed up the design. Hey, God tried, but people blew it, so all the horrible things in this world are our fault. This exercise in self-flagellation is heartbreaking and destructive. It dismisses legitimate questions about the planet's needless waste and suffering, and it lets God, as creator and interventionist, totally off the hook. The British-Canadian philosopher Michael Ruse, who calls intelligent design "an oxymoron," agrees:

> ID [intelligent design] is theology—very bad theology. As soon as you bring God into the world on a daily creative basis, then the theodicy problem—the problem of evil—rears its ugly head. If God works away miraculously to do the very complex, presumably in the name of goodness, then why on earth does God not occasionally get involved miraculously to prevent the very simple with horrendous consequences?[22]

This whole messy affair ultimately brings us back to the ludicrousness of the claim that humans are the product of magic and wizardry, conjured as imperfect, allowed to fumble and fall in dangerous ignorance, and be both responsible for everything that is wrong with the world *and* the center of the universe's attention. We are broken and wretched yet also wonderfully made. These conflicting narratives stretch the brain like taffy.

The truth is before us, all around us, within us. The genetic code, the skeletal frame, the arms, legs, fingers, toes, eyes, ears, jaw, hair, brain, digestive system, respiratory system, reproductive organ, social hierarchies—everything we are—overwhelmingly reveals our primate selves. The proof is right there in front of us: in our microscopes, our mannerisms, our physical makeup, our mirrors. We are a result of billions of years of coding, recoding, dying, surviving, adapting, mutating, developing, and navigating this complex world. Even if some faceless cosmic Other did set all life into motion, he was obviously a lousy planner, he isn't fixing even the smallest of our problems, and he is content to produce children without further support. He is the absentee landlord, the donor sperm, the deadbeat dad. If he exists, what respect or loyalty would he deserve?

These are difficult conversations for many. Realizing that life is fragile and finite in a universe not designed with us in mind can be disconcerting—but there is a tremendous upside. The rejection of mythical creationism frees us to slough off the religiously imposed guilt, shame, and blame for the supposed sins causing our misfortunes and maladies in this natural world. Cancer will remain awful, but humans didn't unleash it as a result of our disobedience. Tsunamis will smash over the shorelines, but human rebellion against God does not surge the deadly tides. Children will tragically die in childbirth but not due to a mother's failed faith. In short, we can stop blaming ourselves for terrible things beyond our control, embrace life as it is, and focus on making this naturally complex and chaotic world better for each other.

Why would acknowledging our primal relatives be considered a cheat to existence? Is life moot and worthless if we are not the product of some cosmic drawing board? Aren't we better off rejecting the insidious claims that sinful humanity is born guilty of everything that is imperfect, tragic, or horrifying in this world? Shouldn't an honest mind be ready to accept overwhelmingly supported evolutionary facts? Isn't acknowledging our connection to all life in the natural world more fulfilling?

I am sure that Christian critics will continue to draw the human animal as a cartoon, but they will be coloring their images with irony, as each stroke of the pencil will be wielded by evolved primate fingers. And as they huff at their own kinship with life in the natural world, they will embrace magical tales of a Perfect Plan gone horribly wrong, blaming humankind for all that is terrible, and fearing dark, supernatural forces seeking to wreak havoc upon their everyday lives.

CHAPTER TWO

The Devil Has Your Number – Paranoia and Panic from the Divinely Protected

The liquid splashed into the laundry room sink. The noxious fumes filled the air, mixing with an atmosphere of urgency and righteous indignation. The woman was a devout Christian—and a relative. The year was 1991, and in the name of Jesus, she was pouring bleach down the kitchen drain.

The Satanic Panic of the 1980s and '90s saw the Devil in every corner of the culture: music, books, films, video games, holidays, children's toys, and yes, even in a gallon of Clorox. (I am coming to the rest of that story.) Parents, pastors, and evangelical politicians had spun themselves into a rabid lather about the evil coming to infect their children, dismantle their Christian nation, and ultimately devolve society into an apocalyptic orgy of moral chaos.

The warnings were dire and eerily specific: Judas Priest albums caused teenagers to commit suicide. He-Man and Skeletor glamorized black magic and idol worship to cartoon-watching children. Yoda was the incarnation of a satanic three-toed beast. My Little Pony cartoons called up the powers of demon necromancers. Dungeons and Dragons transformed game players into actual witches and sorcerers. *The Exorcist* was grafting demons onto moviegoers. Countless unsuspecting people had repressed memories of satanic ritual abuse. Halloween wasn't just the holiday of spooky costumes and sweets but the Devil's Day, his minions lurking to kidnap black cats and sacrifice virgins. Major American corporations were funding the Church of Satan to the tune of millions of dollars, including (and especially) Procter & Gamble—manufacturer of Clorox bleach.

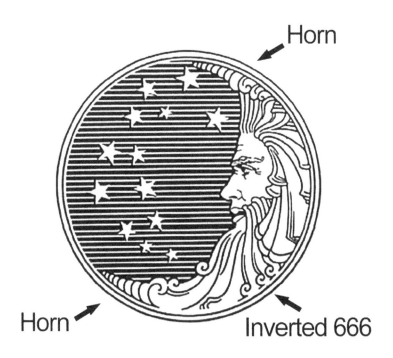

For more than a decade, hordes of indignant Christians boycotted Procter & Gamble over a rumor that P&G's corporate logo was satanic, its "new moon" face containing an inverted 666, devil horns, and thirteen stars. None of the faithful had bothered to research the satanism claim. (Had they done so, they would have learned that the symbol was simply an identifying stamp created by dock workers.)

The warning itself was validation enough, so any purchase of Bounce dryer sheets, Luvs diapers, Bounty paper towels, Tampax tampons, Gillette razors, or Old Spice deodorant would be a *de facto* tithe to the Church of Satan. Christians using a Dove Beauty Bar were literally bathing themselves in the lather of Lucifer. So of course, Clorox belonged in the sewer instead of the laundry cabinet, environment be damned.

Here is a related scenario, and it happened often. If a devout Christian was buying their (non-Clorox) detergent at a retail store and the purchase total rang up at $6.66, it wouldn't be—and still isn't—uncommon for said Christian to wince and scramble for an extra item to change that number. I AM NOT KIDDING. Mainstream Christianity believes that the number 666 is a biblical marker for satanic allegiance in the End Times. It is the *number of the beast*. "No one could buy or sell unless he had this mark, that is, the beast's name or the number that stands for his name" (Rev. 13:17). Hence, even a Walmart receipt could be imbued with dark, destructive powers. "$6.66? Quick! Tack on some breath mints and a Mars bar!"

This apocalyptic paranoia spilled over to retail bar codes, those machine-readable series of lines and numbers used to identify items. Invented back in 1951, they became part of supermarket checkout systems in the 1970s and '80s. The EAN-13 barcode integrates a pattern marking its beginning, middle, and end. Those three patterns were seen by many as sixes—and there it was again: 666.[23] Shopping was getting more dangerous by the day.

More recently, television's KPIX News in San Francisco reported the 2015 story about a Berkeley car buyer horrified about her randomly generated vehicle license plate containing the dreaded three 6's because it was "symbolic of the Devil or the Antichrist."[24] She flatly refused to put the plate on the bumper. This same revulsion is commonly seen in credit card holders horrified at grouped sixes within the numbers of their accounts.

The COVID-19 pandemic saw plenty of doomsayers warning that vaccines and masks were as dangerous as the satanic 666.[25] In March 2021, Georgia Representative Marjorie Taylor Greene called vaccine passports "Biden's mark of the beast."[26] Gab founder Andrew Torba posted a similar warning on Facebook before it was removed, and the social media platform TikTok ultimately had to ban the hashtags #MarkOfTheBeastIsTheCovid19Vaccine and #VaccineIsTheMarkOfTheBeast as the spreading of vaccine disinformation. Christian culture has been suffocated with conspiracy myths about fetal cells, radio trackers, and vaccine mandates as precursors to the arrival of the Antichrist. Yes, even a vaccine designed to save lives represents a sharp needle of evil.

This is the tragicomedy of the Satanic Panic. Believers scan the culture for anything pointy, horny, fanged, creepy, or diabolically coded, and as soon as they feel the first goose bump, they sound their righteous alarms.

I remember many of the warnings in the 1980s and '90s leaning toward the music industry, especially stage-blood-spewing metal bands. But right alongside provocateurs such as Ozzy Osborne and Twisted Sister were ostensibly benign artists such as Simon & Garfunkel and John Denver. This made sense to me at the time. I knew that Satan was sneaky. I understood that he may grind his malevolence through the distortion pedal, but he would just as likely befriend you with doe-eyed innocence.

One of the more intriguing music-related "evils" was a musical tri-tone interval known as the Devil's Chord, a diminished fifth played one fret down. This arrangement of notes, once dubbed *diabolus in musica* (Latin for "devil in music"), creates a sound often considered ugly—a dissonant and uncomfortable kick in the eardrum. The diminished, or flatted, fifth has been around forever, but when metal bands embraced the chord in the 1970s and '80s, fundamentalists figured that their discomfort was being caused by vibrations of a more sinister nature. Pulpit pounders warned that the tritone was satanic and that wicked pied pipers such as Iron Maiden, Alice Cooper, and Black Sabbath were strumming a generation straight toward Hell.

Fear is a common human emotion. Whether we see sixes in logos or perceive eerie voices in the wind, whether it is sensible or irrational, we are all creeped out by something. I am reminded of a 2015 *Smithsonian* article about the science of creepiness,[27] which reveals how the unfamiliar and stigmatized creates an "uncertainty of threat." People get nervous around the strange and unknown. The senses heighten. The brain locks onto the creepy thing, often constructing a sense of sinister agency. Add the religious ingredient, and we can see why it is so common for everyday things to be construed as demonic. After all, all good things come from God (Psalm 16:2), so if something isn't good, it must, by definition, be evil or satanic. The most fearful evangelicals see evil in almost every corner and in almost any scenario, often to comic effect.

Case in point. Back in 2015, my wife, Natalie, and I were on a weekend holiday in Eureka Springs, Arkansas, and caught a magic show. We enjoyed the modest little performance and decided to grab a keepsake in the gift shop: a small, cotton-stuffed voodoo doll, about five inches tall, in black fabric, with tiny stitched facial features. It came with small metal pins and some tongue-in-cheek instructions for use. The directions clearly stated that the doll should be "used only for good" and that bad-faith doll-sticking would return calamity upon the owner. It was obvious that this souvenir was intended as a harmless and amusing token and not a tool for torturing the neighbor who won't return your garden tools. Natalie displayed the voodoo doll on our living room shelf, and every time we looked at it, the trinket brought fond memories.

After the trip, the story of the voodoo doll came up over dinner with a Christian couple from our tennis team, whom I will call Tom and Megan. As they listened to our rundown of the Arkansas weekend, the magic show, and the doll, I suddenly noticed that their smiles had begun to fade. By the time Natalie got to the part about the needles being used only for good, there was a palpable sense of discomfort on their side of the table. Our story ended, and I found myself counting the beats of silence. Tom was suspiciously quiet. Megan looked like she needed another glass of wine. She spoke first. "Why would you keep it?"

I don't think Natalie understood the question at first. My wife, herself a God believer, wasn't perturbed by the doll, so she was nonplussed by Megan's alarm. Natalie said playfully, "It's fun! And we don't use it for evil." There was another long pause, and the obvious suddenly hit me. Tom and Megan believed that we had willfully invited a dangerous Haitian cult into our living room.

A quick digression. I must clarify that voodoo isn't the dark and murderous occult of screaming witchdoctors so often portrayed on television. Originated in Africa, voodoo is a wildly diverse religion that combines African, Catholic, and Native American traditions, links the physical world to a spiritual otherworld, is almost universally peaceful, and—get this—almost never includes dolls. Of course, Natalie and I weren't even thinking about this stuff when we plunked down our fifteen bucks at the gift shop. We just wanted the souvenir.

But Tom and Megan were genuinely disturbed about the doll. This innocuous stitching of cotton and burlap wasn't merely decoration and a conversation piece; it was idolatry. It was devilry. It was a conduit for dark spiritual energy. And it could, in fact, be used as a weapon against one's enemies in the physical world. Needles placed in the head, the chest, and the stomach might produce real calamity for anyone deemed a target. The doll would also serve as a back door for satanic minions looking to possess and oppress. In Tom and Megan's minds, Natalie and I might as well have purchased a live hand grenade. After another moment of nervous questioning, we changed the subject.

Interestingly, Natalie and I saw almost the exact same scenario play out a few years later with another group of religious friends. We were smiling. They were squirming. Our cloth trinket was making them fidget in their seats. This flavor of fear is extremely common in religious cultures. In fact, I would wager that if you showed up on the doorstep of a churchgoing Christian family brandishing a voodoo doll, you would be welcomed inside but the doll would not.

My evangelical years were marked by this fear of icky objects. A Monopoly board made of cardboard and plastic was welcome in the game closet, while a similarly constructed Ouija board would be banished (and possibly burned). Standard six-sided game dice were benign, while twelve-sided Dungeons & Dragons dice were dangerous. Pop and country albums were harmless, while heavy metal albums were imbued with The Beast. A necklace bearing the six-pointed Star

of David was beautiful, while a necklace with a five-pointed penta-
gram was shocking and sinister. The Bible was a beautiful book, while
the Satanic Bible was an unholy and untouchable thing. (Note: The
Satanic Bible is little more than a handbook for Halloweeny atheist
Libertarians penned by an ex-circus performer, and I have never met
an indignant Christian who has actually read the damn thing.)

The Satanic Panic has enthusiastically spilled into the twenty-first
century. Warnings about bat-biting rocker Ozzy Osbourne have
been replaced by panic over rapper Lil Nas X and his blood-dipped
Satan shoes. The '80s conspiracy theory about satanic ritual abuse
at the McMartin preschool has been replaced by Pizzagate, a recent
QAnon myth claiming that Satanists are trafficking child slaves out
of a Washington, DC, pizza joint. Panic about the twentieth-century
Illuminati has been replaced by panic about the twenty-first-century
Illuminati. Tribes constantly vilify their religious, political, and ideological opponents: Protestants declare Catholics satanic. Evangelical
Republicans declare Democrats satanic. Christian nationalists declare
American Muslims, Hindus, seculars, and atheists satanic. Religious
capitalists declare socialists satanic. The National Rifle Association
declares gun restriction advocates satanic. Given the incessant dread
about the Devil, it feels like today's churches could seriously benefit
from some anti-anxiety medication.

But what causes otherwise rational people to lose their terrified
minds? What does their frothing freak-out say about their confidence
in a Great Protector? After all, the Bible is loaded with God's promises
to shield his children from the wiles of Satan. Here are just a few:

- "Fear not, for I am with you." (Isa. 41:10)
- "He is my refuge and my fortress, my God, in whom I trust."
  (Psalm 91:2)

- "He will establish you and guard you against the evil one." (1 Thess. 3:3)

- "The fear of the Lord leads to life, and whoever has it rests satisfied. He will not be visited by harm." (Prov. 19:23)

- "The Lord is on my side; I will not fear. What can man do to me?" (Psalm 118:6)

- "No ill befalls the righteous." (Psalm 121:8)

- "For God gave us a spirit not of fear, but of power and love and self-control." (2 Tim. 1:7)

Apparently, Christians throughout history missed that last verse out of 2 Timothy, their minds consumed with hysteria, the Devil under every rock and over every horizon, the whole planet mere moments from calamity and destruction. Their Christianity enjoys the flowery window dressing of love, joy, peace, and safety, but at the slightest perceived threat, it reveals its foundation: fear. Fear of the unknown. Fear of harm. Fear of evil. Fear of God's wrath. Fear of hellfire.

Suggest this to the faithful, and they will likely knee-jerk in protest. God is love. Jesus is love. No weapon formed against me shall prosper. They might invoke community, the sense of belonging, the joy, love scriptures, the salvation of the soul, and the promise of Heaven. Try this experiment as they describe the warm and sheltering embrace of Kum Ba Yah Jesus: brandish the two-in-one book *Witchcraft for Beginners and Wicca Starter Kit*,[28] and watch their toothy smiles fade into an open-mouthed gasp.

Coming back to the *Smithsonian* science of creepiness study, we see that Christian terror can be sparked by almost any dark, mysterious, dissonant, strangely unusual, or sinister-shaped thing; part of this relates to our evolved tendency to get weirded out over the aforementioned uncertainty of threat. The brains says, "Hey . . . something might be off here," but as the brain can't determine what is actually happening, its alert mechanisms kick in. Unsure and unacclimated, we become uncomfortable, and when we are uncomfortable, we are more inclined to become nervous or afraid. Lock that discomfort within the conspiratorial frame of fundie religions, and you have a recipe for panic. Those strangely illustrated tarot cards become the Devil's Deck. Slayer's strumming of the creepy tritone becomes Satan's chord. Cloth dolls with sewing needles become demonic curse weapons. The strange (and often wonderful) sights and sounds of our world are indicted for the heresies of being unknown, or unpleasant, or simply different. This is the fragile and terrified bubble world for a huge swath of Christians.

This terror of the world helps explain why Jesus culture offers a Christianized version of almost everything to ensure minimal exposure to worldly things. Children need an education? Lock them inside Christian schools. Enjoy pop or rock music? Dial in to contemporary Christian music (CCM) radio stations. Need daycare for the toddler? There is a nursery at the local church. Want to socialize? There is a fellowship dinner on Tuesday. Want to dress with style? Buy cross earrings and a Walk by Faith T-shirt. Need counseling? There are church-sponsored programs such as Divorce Recovery, Addiction Recovery, Grief Recovery, Trauma Recovery, and so on. Want to meet eligible singles? Try ChristianMingle.com.

This closed system of constant reinforcement provides reassurance and an illusion of safety, but it also creates an alternate reality in which the world is perceived through narrow and often distorted lenses. Peering out into the unknown, tribal members can develop wrongheaded and ridiculously tragic notions of the world beyond.

Believers like to boast that they are eagerly engaging secular culture in the name of Jesus, and many certainly do so, but in-group tribalism is actually commanded in the Christian Bible. It instructs, "Do not be yoked together with unbelievers. For what do righteousness and wickedness have in common? Or what fellowship can light have with darkness?"[29] Three verses later, God says, "Come out from them and be separate." This tribal biosphere produces some very problematic consequences because while the tribe itself hunkers down behind its walls, anything and everything beyond becomes a mysterious and often terrifying Other.

Add into the mix a throng of fear-pimping mega-pastors such as John Hagee, Paula White, and Franklin Graham, and you have effectively battened down the church's hatches. Some specific examples:

- The late evangelist Billy Graham declared that "Satan is not only real, but he is far greater than we are, so great that we should have every reason to fear him."[30] An agent of divine confidence was sowing the seeds of cultural terror about the Dark Lord, one side of his mouth saying, "The victory is ours," and the other side whispering, "Be afraid. Be very afraid."

- The website Desiring God warns that Satan uses ten specific strategies to target believers: lying, blinding perceptions, disguises, dark magic, temptation, stealing God's word from the hearts of the faithful, sickness and disease, murder, attacks on missionaries, and false accusations against Christians.[31] Given this barrage of sinister weapons, it is a wonder that Bible believers ever venture out into broad daylight.

- Millions of QAnon conspiracy theorists believe that the American Democratic Party is run by a secret cabal of blood-drinking, sex-trafficking, child-sacrificing Satanists seeking to establish a New World Order in preparation for the Antichrist.

QAnoners claim that vaccines contain hidden radio trackers, Hillary Clinton and Bill Gates drink the blood of babies, an organization of Jewish bankers is setting California wildfires via satellite lasers to panic citizens into climate change legislation, John F. Kennedy Jr. faked his own death to head God's resistance, and any media critical of QAnon is part of a Deep State apocalypse machine. (Lest you think this twenty-first-century Satanic Panic reflects only the wacky fringes, NBC News reported in May 2021 that 20 percent of Americans, most of them white evangelicals, believe some flavor of QAnon conspiracy theories.[32])

How does this brand of irredeemable, brain-melting, Olympic-level stupidity afflict tens of millions of Christians? The answer is simple: *Christianity itself is a conspiracy theory*. Lest you think me mad, let me lay out the basic and biblical foundation of the world's most popular religion.

In the beginning, a cosmic wizard created hundreds of billions of galaxies, yet focused his attention on a single rock in space. On that rock, he conjured a dirt-man and a rib-woman inside an enchanted garden and then allowed an archnemesis (Lucifer's talking serpent) to derail his perfect plan. Cue sixty-six biblical books describing manipulations and murder, heroes in disguises, plots and conquests, temptations and assassins, blessings and curses, marvels and mayhem, divine agents battling devilish foes, and more than one thousand Bible chapters propelling humankind toward a terrifying End Times battle between Christ and the Antichrist—a global battle that kills billions of humans in a blitzkrieg of supernatural doom and death. The story sounds like Tolkien on acid.

The LSD fever dream of the Book of Revelation alone should be enough to raise a skeptical eyebrow. This Bible chapter posits, with a straight face, that one day soon, bloody, fiery hail will rain down upon the planet, that a star named Wormwood will poison Earth's water supply, that two hundred million horsemen will murder a third of the planet's population, and that seven plagues—oozing sores, blood seas, blood rivers, heatwaves, darkness, drought, and earthquakes—will engulf humankind. Also, the Whore of Babylon will ride the Earth upon a scarlet beast with seven heads and ten horns (the heads and horns symbolizing rebellious kings warring against God), and just in case we mortals won't be horrified enough, a Heavenly Warrior dressed in a bloody robe will arrive on a white horse, gather all of the flying birds, and command them to "eat the flesh of kings, generals, and the mighty, of horses and their riders, and the flesh of all people, free and slave, great and small."[33] Amid the chaos, everything will go black, the sky will split open, mountains and islands will move around like chess pieces, and the Antichrist will require all survivors to take the Mark of the Beast to declare their allegiance to Satan before Jesus finally arrives to mop up and take to Heaven all remaining Christians who haven't panicked themselves into heart failure.[34]

On a what-the-fuck meter from one to ten, the Book of Revelation is off the scale. If Christians encountered versions of this story in the Qur'an or the Vedas, they would likely throw those books across the room in disbelief or disgust. Yet billions of evangelicals happily own, embrace, and promote the Christian Bible's crazy climax. Their religion is founded on the story of the white knight and the dark knight, good agents and bad agents, truths and lies, loyalties and betrayals, plans and sabotages, the whole conspiratorial yarn crescendoing into a fantastical, fiery finale. Evil is vanquished. The hero prevails. Roll the final credits.

I have become convinced that Christian culture feeds off of this quixotic hero narrative. They manufacture a scary threat, then anoint themselves the pure-heart crusaders. Ephesians 6 charges believers to "put on the whole armor of God" and gear up for battle. This armor includes the breastplate of righteousness, the shield of faith, the helmet of salvation, the belt of truth, and the sword of the spirit. Christianity is imbued with militarized language, the "army of the Lord" marching in step to "stand against the Devil's schemes."[35] If you are going to war, you need an enemy, even if the threat must be manufactured to suit the conspiracy story. Christ himself declared, "Blessed are those who are persecuted because of righteousness."[36] As such, the good Christian is the persecuted Christian, so danger must be a major component of the machine. Evil is everywhere. It is coming. It is just over that hill. Or in that group. Or with that other religion. Or beyond that border.

Yet these holy warriors, whether they realize it or not, ironically embody the giant in this David-and-Goliath story, having amassed and cloistered an obscene amount of privilege in the United States. Their presidents are sworn in on a Christian Bible. Ninety-one percent of American politicians profess Christianity.[37] Christian television and radio stations broadcast nationwide. More than three hundred thousand Christian churches operate freely in the United States.[38] Christian retailers sell everything from Jesus oil paintings and cross necklaces to Bibleopoly board games. Proselytizers knock on doors without fear of beatings or beheadings. Holidays are decorated in Bible characters and symbols. These self-professed martyrs live in an oppression-free cocoon of obscene entitlement.

So why do so many American evangelicals moan and fret about the persecution they allegedly endure? I suspect three reasons:

1) Beyond all the professions of confidence, Christianity remains

a fear cult: Fear of the Other. Fear of Satan. Fear of danger around every corner of the culture as spiritual dark forces come to steal, kill, and destroy. As such, perceived enemies morph into actual enemies. Who rises up to resist those enemies? The noble heroes. The Lord's Army. This produces a strange clash of attitudes within the Christian church as holy warriors freak out about alleged attackers that God is destined to vanquish. Believers are both victim and victors, quivering in their boots as they declare the battles won.

2) A persecution narrative fuels a shoot-the-messenger scenario that ostensibly insulates Christianity against its critics. Naysayers aren't legitimate, moral people expressing disagreement or concern; they are the enemies of God. Cue the battle trumpets once again. (I am reminded of the famous Ralph Waldo Emerson quote: "Let me never fall into the vulgar mistake of dreaming that I am persecuted whenever I am contradicted."[39])

3) Martyrdom is a convenient way for the powerful to consolidate and retain power. After all, how could a victim ever be an oppressor? Fundamental Christianity expertly flips every challenge to its cultural dominance with Shakespearean acts of victimhood, sometimes actually convinced that the favored majority is the underdog. (As the saying goes, when you're accustomed to privilege, equality feels like oppression.)

The indignant sometimes ask me why I am so vocal in my opposition to theocratic religions, and I am struck by the naivety of the question. If I feel especially snarky, I might respond, "Why do those working to defeat cancer talk so much about cancer?" If I were pressed to be more specific, to go beyond the reasons involving politics and privilege (which is a whole other book), I would say that one of my biggest objections to fundie religions is their untethered moral panic and the damage caused by religious fundamentalism.

In the shadow of the American Satanic Panic, fearful Christians are prime candidates for manipulation, especially by authoritarian savior figures: pastors, prophets, and politicians. Having out-grouped a huge portion of their fellow human beings, many build their bigotries and bad ideas upon theology and conspiracy, passing anti-science, anti-humanity, anti-reality notions down the family tree. In fact, research reveals that religious kids are "less able to distinguish between fantasy and reality compared with their secular counterparts."[40] Primed to see devils in the dark, these kids will become the next generation of QAnons.

If I could go back in time to plead with my fearful, religious self, I would likely say, "The toys are just plastic. The songs are just musical notes. The bleach is just cleaner. Stop scanning so desperately for the bad and beastly, unlock your doors and venture out into the sun, meet the people and discover the world you have so sadly misunderstood, and realize that life is too short and precious to spend it in terror of your own shadow."

Irrational fears often have tragic consequences. The benign seems threatening. The abnormal seems reasonable. The crazy seems sane. And as the next chapter reveals, many victims of magical religious claims are young, trusting, and very impressionable children.

CHAPTER THREE
Strange Passion –
Easter Torture Theater

It was Easter weekend. I was driving by a local Baptist church when I noticed a cluster of costumed children in the parking lot. About half were dressed as Roman guards, complete with plastic swords, and they were pointing and shouting . . . at Jesus. A child actor was dressed as Christ in white rags, wearing a crown of thorns and carrying a faux cross. Other children in biblical robes stood at the outer rim of the scene, and an adult audience, presumably parents, stood at a distance. Obviously, this was an Easter play. The Passion Play.

In Christianity, the Passion refers to the suffering of Christ at his crucifixion. The word *passion* comes from the Latin verb *patior, passus sum*, which translates to "to suffer, bear, endure." It is common for Christian churches to reenact key moments leading to—and through—the execution of their savior.

Jesus triumphantly enters Jerusalem as the adoring crowd honors him with palm leaves (which explains why Christians now celebrate Palm Sunday). Mary anoints him with oil. He shares a meal with the disciples at the Last Supper. Judas the betrayer kisses him. He is arrested, tried in the court of Pontius Pilate, scourged to a bloody pulp, nailed to a cross erected between two thieves, entombed, and ultimately resurrected by God. Christ's torture and execution ostensibly provided a blood atonement for all of humankind, his sacrifice revered and celebrated by billions, with believers shouting on every Easter holiday that "He is risen!"

This execution-as-entertainment scenario is played out yearly around the world, its tastelessness masked in a veil of virtue. Sure, the scene is bloody and provocative, but it is a noble "true" story that—of course—must be reenacted in a Tulsa parking lot.

Speaking of reenactments, in my 2015 book, *Sacred Cows*, I write about the jaw-droppingly awful Easter ritual in the Philippines, where, on every Good Friday for thirty-four years (as of this writing), a man named Ruben Enaje has had himself literally nailed to a cross. He even keeps the nails in a jar year-round. (He had to cancel his performance in 2021 because of the COVID-19 pandemic.) This painful tradition has turned his village of Pampanga into a yearly tourist attraction—complete with gift shops. Tragically, Ruben seems to have misunderstood the whole point of Jesus's crucifixion. If you believe the Bible, Christ already atoned for sin, and humans are off the hook.

Perhaps the most famous (and certainly profitable) example of the Passion Play is Mel Gibson's 2004 film, *The Passion of the Christ*, which remains the highest-grossing Christian film of all time. Upon its release, this hard-R gorefest was lauded by Christian churches everywhere—until Gibson crucified his own reputation with alleged domestic violence, racist rants, and a drunk driving arrest, during which he vomited the anti-Semitic claim that "the Jews are responsible for all the wars in the world."

Gibson's fall from grace resulted in a conspicuous, nervous silence from the churches that embraced him almost two decades ago, but the Passion story continues to be told in films, plays, books, and even puppet shows. Yes, puppet shows, a recent example being Holy Land Christian Theater in Paradise, Pennsylvania, in which marionettes pinned Jesus to his cross.

We can smirk at Christian audiences lining up for forty-five minutes of puppet murder, but there is a more serious underlying issue here. Many of these macabre plays involve children.

When I was a devout believer, I probably wouldn't have blinked if my church had organized a children's reenactment of the crucifixion. The Christ/cross story had been branded into my consciousness by parents, Sunday teachers, vacation bible schools, my entire culture. It was absolutely normal for a five-year-old to be surrounded by portraits and statues of an agonized man with spikes pounded through his bones—a pre-corpse hanging and heaving as blood and water oozed from the spear wound in his side. Very often, pastor podiums would stand in the shadow of a large cross mounted on the stage wall behind them. Today, I wonder how my family would have reacted if their church had removed that cross and mounted an electric chair, a cyanide canister, or a noose over the baptismal.

On that note, let's do an experiment. Let us reimagine the Passion Play as performed by those earnest and eager Baptist kids, but let's use a noose instead of the cross.

As Jesus is put on trial before Pilate, the young actors in the circle shout, "Hang him! Hang him!" The eleven-year-old Jesus is dragged by the mob toward the gallows, its rope already looped and swaying ominously in the breeze. Bruised and staggering, the Jesus child reaches the platform as the crowd taunts and jeers, eagerly anticipating the snap of his neck. There is wild applause as the noose is looped and tightened around the boy's throat, the hooded executioner standing nearby with his fingers on the trapdoor handle. The kids continue to scream, "Hang him! Hang him!" as their parents watch adoringly. Torturous moments pass . . . then the trapdoor spills the Jesus child six feet before jerking his body to a halt, a nearby foley artist breaking a twig to simulate a snapping spine. The "corpse" is lowered to the ground, placed on a stretcher, and discarded behind a Styrofoam stone door as his mother wails with grief. Some exposition is given to time-lapse the Friday-to-Sunday waiting period, and then the child— with his neck permanently scarred from the rope—emerges to forgive his murderers.

How creepy is this scenario? And what makes it any different from the accepted version with the cross?

I kick myself for not noticing sooner the insanity of organizing a children's murder play, but I had been indoctrinated to blindly accept the cross as a symbol of goodness, hope, light, and love. Easter pageants featuring these types of reenactments were as normal as nativity scenes on Christmas, and crosses were ubiquitous: Crosses on steeples. On church walls. In oil paintings. In hospital rooms. Christian culture was peppered with cross necklaces, earrings, bracelets, vehicle decals, picture frames, T-shirts, tattoos, coffee mugs, album covers, even hard candy. Especially in the Bible Belt, throw a stone in any direction, and you will probably hit a cross.

The ingenuity of retailers is pretty impressive, as even nonreligious companies sell their wares to the Easter masses. The Hershey Company offers edible chocolate crosses. Chocolate Fantasies sells crucifixion lollipops, complete with a chocolate Jesus melted to the cross. The Oriental Trading Company sells the popular Testamints, breath mints featuring an embossed cross wrapped in a scripture verse. Websites such as Etsy and Pinterest feature special baking molds for cross-shaped cakes, cookies, and pastries. Imagine baking a lethal injection table or a firing squad bullet for the kids, folks.

For sheer cult theater, it is hard to beat the Easter display at Trinity Baptist Church in Indian Land, South Carolina, which posted a video of its "blood fountain."[41]

 Rick Robin Cope was live. ...
April 4 · 🌐

Thank you Jesus for the Blood ! 💧 💧

 3K   33 Comments 186K Views

The photograph doesn't do it justice, but yes, crimson-dyed water flows from the cross's nail holes into a blood pool. You can find a video of it on Facebook. The only thing missing from the display is Vlad Dracula sucking the arterial juice through a straw.

Now, where you and I might expect a healthy number of #WTF responses to this display, the comments section is instead a terrifying series of bumper-sticker affirmations: "The blood." "Thank you Lord Jesus for your shed blood!" "Thank you for the blood!" Several commenters used blood-droplet emojis to express their awe and gratitude.

Beyond the blood-drunk Christian Old Testament, Christianity eagerly steeps itself in blood symbolism. Crack open a Christian hymnal or worship album, and you are immediately covered in crimson:

> Are you washed in the blood?
> In the soul cleansing blood of the Lamb?
> Are your garments spotless, are they white as snow?
> Are you washed in the blood of the Lamb?[42]

Of course, this cleansing blood originated at the "The Old Rugged Cross," the classic hymn celebrating the "emblem of suffering and shame,"[43] our shame adding another troubling clot to the bloody pool. Creepier still is the lyric, "I will cling to the old rugged cross," which conjures images of believers clutching the bloody wood in blame for Christ's beautiful-yet-horrible execution. Worthy of damnation in a torturous Hell, all of humankind—past, present, and future—is culpable for the murder of God. (If I may digress, I have questions about how an invincible deity can be killed. The Passion story would be more accurately summed up with the tagline "Jesus had a really shitty weekend for your sins.")

Yet the cross has moved from a symbol of agony and execution to a symbol of cleansing and love. Forget the spikes, the hammering, the screams and spearing and spitting and sadism. Jesus bled redemption from his perfect veins, and of course, his is a lovely story that should be eagerly told to wide-eyed children.

I recently saw a tweet by a guy named Carl,[44] which perfectly sums up the madness:

 CarlP

I can't believe I used to sing about being washed in blood like it was totally normal.

9:32 PM · Mar 27, 2021 · Twitter for Android

When did blood magic become normalized in the public consciousness? And why are Christianity's blood rituals on the safe end of a huge double standard regarding other faiths and traditions?

I would love to invite my Christian friends into a non-Christian temple themed around a different god (let's call him Bran, Bringer of Light), with a hidden camera rolling. Beyond the main platform would be a randomly chosen execution device; let's use the guillotine in our example. Richly colored oil paintings of the headless Bran would adorn the walls and halls. Songbooks would rhyme catchy phrases about his wounds and his sacrifice. Congregants would chant, sing, and pray to be covered in the blood of Bran. Priests would wax in lofty love language, thinly disguising threats to the noncompliant: "Bran loves you, but failure to accept his blood will result in eternal pain and punishment." Blood sermons, blood songs, blood symbols, and blood rituals honoring Bran would be taught to six-year-olds. The kids would be trained to plead the blood, to be washed in the blood, to draw power from the blood. Every month, the church body would cannibalize

Bran, Bringer of Light, by drinking him from communion cups. "What can wash away my sin? What can make me whole again? Nothing but the blood of Bran."

Panicking at the exit door, the Christians would be calling down Jesus's blood to protect them from Bran's blood, completely blind to the irony that they would still be begging to be showered in blood!

How did we get here?

First, it is important to acknowledge that Christianity's origins are rooted in a primitive and often barbaric era of human history, a time when animal throats were slashed to appease the spirits, when burnt-flesh offerings sent sickening smoke toward the nostrils of the gods, when execution theater was so normalized that Colosseum crowds cheered the lions eating the victims.

Second, it is critical to acknowledge that Jesus wasn't the first dying-and-rising god. Long before Christianity, mythologies spun similar tales of deaths and resurrections, passions and sacrifices, these hero gods forming genre faiths that appealed to the masses. The Christian Christ was predated by interchangeable gods that were miraculously born (sometimes even of virgins), had human characteristics (walking and talking as men), commanded symbolic water rituals (baptism), offered family and group memberships (children of God), died dramatically for a higher purpose (atonement, destiny), and rose again to promise a posthumous afterlife for the faithful (Heaven).

Centuries before Christianity, the Egyptian god Osiris assumed a mortal body, was murdered and dismembered, and was reconstituted to rule from a higher realm.[45] While Christ was resurrected on the third day, Osiris was resurrected on the fifth and crowned as a king; his passion was honored by the faithful in rituals.[46] Tales of the dead-and-resurrected

Osiris were found inscribed on the Egyptian pyramids, the oldest known depictions dating back to 2300 BCE—more than two thousand years before Jesus's Passion was alleged to have happened.[47] Interestingly, the worship of Osiris in the Roman Period fell out of fashion during the rise of Christianity, one genre overtaking another.

Other early dying-and-rising gods include the Mesopotamian goddess Inanna, her death-by-crucifixion story inscribed on clay tablets more than one thousand years before the beginning of Christianity.[48] Inanna rose on the third day. Romulus, the mythical first king of Rome, was said to be a god who assumed mortal form from a virgin birth. Legend has it that Romulus traveled with disciples before being executed by the Roman Senate, returned in divine form, and just like Jesus, ascended to Heaven.[49] Hercules, another popular Roman god, was said to have died, risen from the dead, and—thanks to an apotheosis (divination) by Zeus—ascended to Olympus in all his glory. The grand stories of Hercules date back to 1300 BCE.[50]

I will leave the detailed examinations to the historians, but there is no doubt that even a cursory glance at the ancient past reveals a litany of gods who assumed human form, did heroic deeds, died a dramatic and often gruesome death, and blew the doors off of their earthly tombs in a cascade of supernatural power. Whatever Jesus Christ is or isn't, he certainly isn't anything new. Beyond the spears, swords, and savage deaths of history's gods lies the irony of twenty-first-century Christians mock-executing their own savior while remaining ignorant or dismissive of all the others.

If child actors dragged a costumed Inanna to the cross as the mobs cried out for blood, there is no doubt the horrified parents and Baptist church staff would immediately call a halt to such macabre theater. Killing Jesus, however, is just fine. Crucify him. Nail him to the wood.

Scream and shout and sneer and spit. Let his blood spill. Let him cry to Heaven to ask, "Why hast thou forsaken me?" Let his lungs heave out a final breath before his head collapses to his chest. Let him be brought down and tucked inside the rocks so that he can appear thereafter, remind us of our sin, and then forgive us for it.

Perhaps this is the most troubling thing about Christianity's "love" message. It is constructed upon a foundation of blame, shame, guilt, and threats of torture. According to the Bible, all of humankind was "brought forth in iniquity," a "slave to sin," "astray from birth." "There is no one righteous, not even one." Without divine intervention, those not redeemed from their own humanity will be "thrown into the lake of fire," where there will be "wailing and gnashing of teeth."[51]

Christians often get misty-eyed over the Bible's many love verses, but under all the sweetness and light lies the darker dogma: the claim that the entire human race is so filthy and wicked that it deserves the agony of Hell. Born broken, people have inherited the sins of Adam and are as guilty for Jesus's crucifixion as the Roman soldiers who pounded the spikes. As the classic hymn "Unworthy" goes:

> Unworthy am I of the grace that He gave,
> Unworthy to hold to his hand;
> Amazed that a King would reach down to a slave,
> This love I cannot understand.[52]

Sure, the celebrity pastors and modern churches have softened Hell theology for the masses, morphing fire and brimstone into a less horrifying separation-from-God scenario, but the scriptures remain clear, and Christianity largely follows the party line that we are unworthy and that we must get our worth from Another. This tragic claim automatically diminishes self-worth, and when examined closely, looks suspiciously like the language of abusers. God says the following:

- Profess your allegiance to me—or else.
- You are broken. You need me to fix you.
- You don't deserve me. I am doing you a favor. Be grateful I didn't let you rot.
- Make sure I get all the focus and attention. Validate me always.
- If you are hurt, even by my hand, it is your own fault.
- Whatever happens, don't dare leave me, or you will be sorry.

How tragic that the child actors in that passion play were essentially brainwashed to celebrate the abusive home that is the fundamentalist Christian church. Instead of being validated as precious human beings deserving of goodness, safety, love, value, and purpose on their own terms, these indoctrinated kids have been bequeathed to their parents' god, acting out compulsory love under threat, locked inside narrow religious walls . . . the battered bride of Christ.

Perhaps one day, these young people will grow to question the bizarre theater of that Easter weekend in 2021. Maybe they will lament the memory of swords and spikes in their hands, aghast that anyone would need—or want—to reenact a crime scene so they might be showered in blood. Beyond all of that, maybe they will come to reject the high-control blood cult of fundamentalist Christianity, finally embracing their own innate worth, breathing the oxygen of freedom, and encouraging their own children to do the same.

Sadly, though, Christianity will likely remain obsessed with the power of the blood, and as they are awash in crimson on the outside, they will also eagerly accept the blood of Jesus within.

CHAPTER FOUR
Eat Jesus – The Creepy, Culty Ritual of Communion

"While they were eating, Jesus took bread, and when he had given thanks, he broke it and gave it to his disciples, saying, 'Take and eat; this is my body.' Then he took a cup, and when he had given thanks, he gave it to them saying, 'Drink from it, all of you. This is my blood of the covenant, which is poured out for many for the forgiveness of sins.'"[53]

The Last Supper remains one of the most iconic and widely referenced stories from the Christian Bible, and understandably so. The stage is being set for a climax to the thirty-three-year Jesus story. The players are gathered. There is enjoyment, music, and merriment. Yet seated at the table are not one but two betrayers, both of whom are exposed by Christ in those fateful moments. Jesus predicts aloud that the apostle Peter will vehemently deny him no fewer than three times to save his own skin, and more critically, he marks Judas as the traitor who will damn his own soul for thirty pieces of silver (in today's currency, a mere few hundred bucks).[54]

The Last Supper, by Leonardo da Vinci

The setting for this high drama is a simple dinner, where, as depicted throughout the centuries, all participants are seated at half of the table. (I am reminded of that Last Supper joke: Hey! Everyone on this side if you want to be in the photo!) Of course, if we see the Last Supper as a stage play and the participants as heroes and villains, paintings such as the 1490 Leonardo da Vinci masterpiece make a lot more sense. The characters are all visible, all maneuvering, all thinking and whispering and speaking and acting. Of course, the long table is set with bread and wine. Significant things are happening by the minute, the entire Passover meal symbolic of the sacrificial lamb's blood that will allow God's chosen people to escape the Angel of Death.

Marking this blood symbolism are the bizarre instructions of Matthew 26: "Take and eat; this is my body. . . . Drink from [the cup], all of you. This is my blood of the covenant."

There are some chronological problems with the story, as the Gospels disagree on the order of events. As written in Matthew, Mark, and John, Christ predicts his betrayal before this communion, while in

Luke the prediction comes after communion. The books of the New Testament also disagree on the order of communion: In Matthew and Mark the bread comes before the wine, in Luke the wine comes before the bread, and there is no mention of communion whatsoever in John.[55] There are other inconsistencies and conflicts, such as the details of Peter's denial and the words spoken by Christ, but I don't want to digress too far from the communion ritual itself, a ritual that Jesus commanded and that the Christian church has embedded into its doctrines and customs. Jesus said, Do this in remembrance of me, and Christianity obliged.

I remember when I was a kid sitting in the pew at "big church," I felt a sense of real excitement on Communion Sunday. The deacons would stack communion trays on the stage, which meant only one thing to me: snacks! In retrospect, I am still not sure if my enthusiasm was about being served a thimble-sized glass of Welch's grape juice and a saltine, or if it was relief that the overlong sermon would end a few minutes early. In those moments I wasn't thinking about flesh and blood, nor did I possess the maturity or perspective to properly understand what was happening.

As I grew to adulthood, however, I was fully aware of what the food represented, and still I ingested the fake blood and faux flesh without hesitation. I ate my savior, and the practice seemed perfectly normal, even empowering. I felt a bit holier, more sanctified, more worthy. I had already come to see myself as a crusader in God's army, so perhaps communion served to fortify me against the forces of evil. I stood at my pew, chanted the incantation, and along with the whole congregation, consumed a piece of God.

Now, it is fair to point out that Baptists—and most protestant churches—are up front about serving crackers and juice, which merely *symbolize* flesh and blood, but this vampiristic sacrament is something that Christians would reject in another context. (Hey, Steve, let's pretend these wafers are the flesh of your late Uncle Joey and eat him on his birthday.)

Christian congregations are untroubled by standing to their feet, raising a glass of pretend plasma, waiting for a pastor to say drink up, and ghoulishly knocking back some flavored Jesus. Would they be so eager to engage if the juice and crackers represented the blood and body of Allah, Krishna, or Zeus, or would the devout consider communion ridiculous and macabre in those other contexts?

The Catholic Church sets the gold standard for communion, where the practice is better known as the Eucharist (based on the Greek εὐχαριστία, which translates as "thanksgiving"). Not content to consume Jesus merely symbolically, Catholics believe in the divine miracle of transubstantiation, which means that a "substantial conversion" occurs when juice and bread turn into the *actual blood and flesh* of Christ.[56] In other words, the planet's largest religious institution promotes and practices cannibalism.

I was never a Catholic. My Christian family saw Catholicism as a false faith, even though it is considered a branch of Christianity, is based on the Bible, and embraces a literal Christ in its theology. In the protestant Baptist and Assembly of God churches, our teachings were sound; those of the Catholic Church were unsound. We had access to Jesus; Catholics were stuck praying to Mary and the saints. Our Sunday services and customs were warm and engaging; theirs were stilted and lifeless. Our communion was perfectly reasonable; theirs was eerily culty. (Protestant teetotalers also winced at the fact that Catholics used real alcoholic wine.)

Catholicism does ramp up the freak factor on many fronts. Catholic history and tradition are *loaded* with the bizarre: the miracle of stigmata (spontaneous bleeding at the points of crucified Jesus's wounds), knotted purity belts, exorcisms, throat blessings, weeping yard Madonnas, and the chantings of constipated bishops dressed like eleventh-century chess pieces. I have become fascinated by this mysterious culture of rosary beads and incense burners, rites and cathedrals, priests and papals. Above all, I am obsessed with transubstantiation. If twenty-one million American Catholics believe they are actually eating and drinking Jesus,[57] how—logistically—does this "miracle" happen?

I began my quest to answer this question by consulting an article penned by Father Francis J. Ripley, helpfully titled, "Transubstantiation for Beginners," which provides this clear-as-mud explanation:

- The changing of crackers and wine into flesh and blood is much like the turning of day into night, the change of a positive element "expressed negatively" as one thing transitioning to another.

- Conversion requires "two positive extremes" of things related to each other. It is not a miracle for water to merely transform into steam. A true miracle is water turning into wine, or in the case of communion, wine turning into blood.

- The original substance "must in some manner cease to exist."

- "All that substance sustains, the things which inhere in it, we call by the technical name of accidents. We cannot touch, see, taste, feel, measure, analyze, smell, or otherwise directly experience substance. Only by knowing the accidents do we know it. So we sometimes call the accidents the appearances."[58]

Father Ripley's five-thousand-word screed raises more questions than answers. I read it a second time, and as far as I could tell, between the one-minus-one-equals-Jesus lines of reasoning, his proof boiled down to: believe it because it's true. Ask the Bible. And the Pope. This was profoundly unsatisfying. I dug deeper.

Father William Saunders, at the Catholic Education Resource Center, offers this clarification:

> By the will of the Father, the word of the Holy Spirit, and priest-hood of Jesus entrusted to His ordained priests, and through the words of consecration, that bread and wine is transformed into the Body and Blood of Jesus. Yes, the bread and wine do not change in characteristics; they will look the same, taste and smell the same, and hold the same shape. However, the reality, "the what it is," the substance does change. We do not receive bread and wine; we receive the Body and Blood of Christ.[59]

Father Saunders had just stated in the same breath that:

- the bread and wine are transformed;
- the bread and wine do not change in characteristics; and
- the substance transforms without transforming.

Exasperated, I consulted the Q&A page of the United States Conference of Catholic Bishops. I soon regretted it. Monsignor William Pay sounded just like those I had read before: "Christ's presence in the Eucharist is unique in that, even though the consecrated bread and wine truly are in substance the Body and Blood of Christ, they have none of the accidents or characteristics of a human body, but only those of bread and wine."[60]

In other words, yeah, it is literal flesh and blood, but it bears absolutely no material properties of flesh and blood. By this standard, I could list a paddleboat for sale on *Auto Trader* under the header "New Lexus!" The boat would have none of the properties or characteristics of the Lexus (because it had transformed without being transformed), but it would still be a Lexus.

Have the wafer-thin claims about transubstantiation ever been scientifically tested? I mean, it's a damn miracle, so *something* should change. Lo and behold, I discovered a study conducted by—wait for it—the Association of Raëlian Scientists in Las Vegas. Raëlianism is a UFO cult that claims that humanity was created by extraterrestrials known as the Elohim. If that name sounds strangely connected to the Abrahamic god, you will be interested to learn that Raëlians don't believe in gods but, rather, translate Elohim as "sky messengers," immortal aliens with green skin and almond-shaped eyes. Those aliens are allegedly using a supercomputer to track our DNA so that humans can be reanimated after death to face judgment in an alien court. Wait! Don't leave! I'm getting to a legitimate point!

Devout Raëlians Damien Marsic (a molecular scientist at Switzerland's Porton Biologics) and Mehran Sam (a biologist who once worked at Harvard) were dubious about the Catholic Church's claim of transubstantiation, so they subjected communion crackers to DNA analysis. Sure, the whole bug-eyed green men story gives us good reason to take Marsic and Sam with a grain of salt, but their lab results are interesting, and as it is the only such study I could find, let's take a look at their results.

The team collected cell samples from "consecrated hosts" (humans) in five Catholic Churches throughout the United States and Canada. They extracted DNA from these cells as well as DNA from altar bread samples purchased at a church supply store. Elaborate tests of "consecrated wafers" revealed no human DNA that couldn't be otherwise explained by simple handling.[61] In other words, nothing in the bread had transformed into flesh. Marsic and Sam's findings provide an interesting refutation to the Church's supernatural claims. Again, I am not saying we should blindly accept the word of Raëlians, but it is just fine to watch their experiment with interest.

Of course, those primed to believe in magical transformations will be untroubled by any laboratory result. Aside from peeling open someone's esophagus for real-time observation, the claim of a bread-to-body metamorphosis during swallowing remains conveniently unfalsifiable. Besides, since the Church has already declared that Jesus's flesh and blood disguise themselves as food, testing seems moot.

Hell, the Church already admits that the wafers are simple food, as it recently enforced Catholic canon law forbidding gluten-free crackers.[62] Only fresh, unleavened bread made from pure wheat is acceptable to God, and pure wheat bread involves gluten. (Notice how the Vatican is untroubled by the eating of flesh but freaks out over a food protein. This is what superstition does to people.)

Throughout Christian culture, the communion scenario—the chants, the crimson chalices, the cannibalism—is rooted in the tragic belief that God looked at his children with a straight face and said, "Eat me." The edibles can be symbolic or deemed miraculously real, but the ritual remains yet another creepy example of how superstitions encourage batshittery in otherwise reasonable people.

Ask those same people which of the gospels command the Eucharist, and they will likely shrug. Ask them who authored Matthew, Mark, and Luke and they will likely respond, "Duh. It's Matthew, Mark, and Luke," which reveals again how little mainstream Christians know about their own Bible. The New Testament Gospels were penned long decades after the alleged life and death of Christ.[63] They are not chronologically ordered (Mark was written before Matthew). Despite the later-added titles (such as "According to Matthew"), authorship has never been proven, and some of the books—Mark, for example— appear to have two, even three different authors.[64]

Add the fact that the Bible is stacked with wild tales about garden conjurings, donkeys that argue in Hebrew, nine-hundred-year-old men, sea monsters, magic mud, seven-headed dragons, ghost sex, an Earth with corners, murder bears, talking shrubbery, golden hemorrhoids (no kidding), and supermen who gain power based on hair length, and we have some pretty good reasons to be skeptical about the whole cannibalism command.

Yet skepticism isn't the order of the day in Christian faith culture. The god of mysterious ways wants his children to eat and drink the flesh and blood because the Bible tells them so. In other words, over the centuries, billions of Christians have blindly obeyed a doomed godman's dinner demands. For them, eating flesh and drinking blood, even symbolically, is reasonable. It is normal. It is written. God doesn't merely want to enter your heart. He would like a place in your stomach as well.

Welcome to fundamental religion. Hook, line, and sinker, fundamentalist Christians have heard the call to cannibalism and literally swallowed it whole.

CHAPTER FIVE

Look to the East – Thoughts on the Second Coming of Christ

My grandmother lived a long, full life. She died in 2004 at the age of ninety-one. Grandma was the quintessential granny. Vintage gray hair. Rocking chair. Crochet needles. A teetering sweet-old-lady soprano when she spoke. She had costume jewelry on the dresser, cowboy blues in her record collection, and furniture upholstered in gaudy flowers.

Grandma carried the endearing innocence of an uncomplicated life, one that rarely interacted with the messy outside world. Her world was family—the kids and grandkids—and for a child like me, a day at Grandma's house was like a day at the chocolate factory. Without fail, there were sweets on the table, cartoons on the television, and toys in the closet. Houseguests napped in knitted blankets colored like rainbows. It all sounds sticky-sweet, but these are my memories of Grandma.

Her death wasn't unexpected. Near the end, her mind had started to slip away, and finally, the rest of her body followed. The funeral included a short graveside service on a pleasant Sunday in March. The programs were printed. The speakers were scheduled. The weather was beautiful.

In my entire life, I had never seen Grandma read the Bible. She never attended church. Her Christianity was always assumed, but if she had a Christian faith, she kept it to herself. If she owned a Bible, I never saw it. If she prayed, she did it beyond anyone's view. In retrospect, I can't think of a single moment when my grandmother seemed even remotely interested in religion. Still, a Christian funeral was a foregone conclusion. It's not like sweet little Granny would be sent to her reward by a Muslim imam or Hindu priest. Grandma was the product of red-state, Bible-banging Oklahoma, and doggone it, if she was going to meet anyone in the Hereafter, it was going to be Jesus.

At the gravesite, Grandma's casket was front and center, draped in the typical oversized funeral flowers. Some constipated suit offered his platitudes and the required funeral verses: I go and prepare a place for you. O death, where is thy sting? The one who believes in me will live, even though they die. (These types of ceremonies are always homogenous, like someone mail-ordered them from The Funeral Store.) The sterile, line-item sermon clashed with the raw nerves of my family's grief, but the message adequately told the story. Grandma was loved. She will be missed. We will see her again in Heaven.

As the service began, I noticed that my mother looked agitated. Twitchy. And she wasn't the only one. I whispered to my sister, "What's the problem?" Beth responded, "Grandma is facing the wrong way." I took a moment to digest this, and then I decided to question Mom directly. Distressed, she pointed to the casket. "She's facing west."

My face went blank. I wasn't processing. My eyes blinked up toward Grandma.

"She's supposed to be facing *east*," Mom protested. "They're not going to bury her facing west, are they? Someone needs to tell the funeral people *not to bury her facing west!*"

An awkward moment passed. I said nothing and walked back to my chair. My head was spinning, which was perhaps why I wasn't connecting my family's alarm to the famous Bible passage of Matthew 24:27: "For as lightning that comes from the east is visible even in the west, so will be the coming of the Son of Man."

This "coming" refers to the Second Coming, the Rapture, the grand return of Christ to gather up his children and lead them into eternity. Scripture declares that a heavenly horn will sound, the sky will transform into a lovely Thomas Kinkaid painting, Jesus will appear with arms outstretched, and Christians—dead and alive—will rocket upward for a huge family reunion in the clouds. "For the Lord himself will come down from Heaven, with a loud command, with the voice of the archangel and with the trumpet call of God, and the dead in Christ shall rise first."[65]

If we are to understand my mother's concern, we must understand that the last part of that verse is critical: *The dead in Christ shall rise first*. Per scripture, the graves of the fallen faithful will open, the saints will rise, and as Jesus will be coming like lightning from the east, it is apparently very important to face dead Christians toward the Big Event. It's for this reason that cemeteries usually orient the graves of Christians eastward, including the headstones. (Next time you are at a graveyard, look around and see for yourself.) Proper casket direction is a "thing" in Christian culture. This fact was explained to me in whispers under the gravesite tent, and I caught myself smirking. I also thought I heard a chuckle from inside Grandma's casket. She knew a good joke when she heard one.

Within minutes, the funeral staff had patted down my family's ruffled feathers, and after the final prayer, cemetery workers dutifully spun Grandma 180 degrees before lowering her into the ground. At the

Rapture, dear Granny will be properly pointed with eyes on the prize.

Driving home, I found myself pondering the day's little crisis. I imagined the trumpet sounding, the skies parting, Christ arriving, and the unlucky billions who had been buried facing the wrong direction. Beyond the logistical questions played the tragicomedy of my family's concern. I was still a Christian at the time, and I understood the lightning metaphor's message that the flash itself would illuminate everything in all directions, but Mom had been genuinely worried that Jesus would skip over resurrected saints if he could only see the backs of their heads.

The more we examine this scenario, the more confusing it becomes, and as you and I are professed skeptics and critical thinkers, I think we owe it to ourselves to take a closer look.

Mainly, we have the directional dilemma. My mother was operating with the expectation that Christ would appear in the east in relation to our geographical coordinates in the United States. Yet one would assume that Jesus would arrive near his biblical focal point, Jerusalem, the great city where he was once greeted with palm leaves and fanfare. Jerusalem is iconic, long serving as an allegory for the Christian church itself, the Holy City where Christ died, was resurrected, and bade farewell at the Ascension. In this light, Jerusalem makes a hell of a lot more sense than Tulsa, Oklahoma.

Still, while a Jerusalem return would still qualify as east, we are talking about an event that would take place almost seven thousand miles away, on the other side of the globe. I suppose Christ could drift in the exosphere 120,000 miles above, but one still wonders 1) how visible he would be, and 2) where he would draw the east/west line. In fact, that dividing line remains an unsolvable problem on several fronts:

If Jerusalem is, in fact, the Rapture's focal point, what happens to the Christians buried (and facing) further east, in Jordan, India, Russia, and so on? From their vantage, Jesus would arrive from the west. South Africans and others would have to gaze north. Those in Norway and Finland would be looking due south. North and South Americans would be pretty much blind to the whole thing. What happens if the Second Coming occurs and those billions miss it (or worse, if the Second Coming misses them)?

What if Ground Zero isn't Jerusalem? What if Jesus does, in fact, decide to appear at the fenceline of Tulsa's Memorial Cemetery? Grandma, being pointed eastward, would be safe, but as Christ would have to be facing *west* to see her, Oklahoma towns behind him, such as Inola and Locust Grove, would be in Jesus's blind spot. What about those east of our state line, in Arkansas, Kentucky, and New York? Whole countries would be hosed, from Morocco to France to (ironically) Israel.

Let's arbitrarily pick any fixed point on the planet. If Jesus arrives in all his glory, are we expected to believe that an all-seeing god would be directionally blind? The Bible declares that God "knows everything,"[66] even the numbers of hairs on our heads, and that "no creature is hidden from his sight." God sees the universe. He sees through time. He "looks to the ends of the earth and sees everything under the heavens." Given Jesus's omniscience, casket orientation shouldn't be a problem. Certainly, it is not unreasonable to expect Christ to simply glance around for anyone he might have missed. After all, would an earthly parent on the hunt for a missing child declare a shoulder turn too inconvenient?

Next, we are left to wonder about those who died horrible deaths through bodily violence. If a swimmer had lost a leg to a Great White and died, would Christ first regenerate the amputated limb, or would a one-legged Christian fly out of his grave? What about those whose bodies were mangled in other terrible ways, from animal attacks and car accidents to serial killers and industrial accidents? (I suppose that if you already believe God will reverse the rot, undo the bodily decay, purge the worms, and rebuild a decomposed body before levitating it into the atmosphere, the mangling issue won't be a problem.)

Finally, we have the huge number of cremated Christians. Would all existing urns explode as physical bodies returned? What about cremains long ago scattered on sentimental resting places, such as wooded fields, snowy mountains, various lakes and oceans? If the classic rock group Kansas was correct that we are merely dust in the wind, would globs of ash become sentient and fly into the sky? What about the long-ago cremated Christians whose granules of calcium phosphates, sodium, potassium, sulfur, and carbon have already been reconstituted into other things? What about those people who had been instantly vaporized in the large furnaces of volcanic eruptions and thermonuclear blasts?

So many questions. In fact, I would wager that many of my readers will expose other problems I haven't yet considered. Yet my biggest sticking point is not about Rapture logistics. More than anything else, I am struck by how easily, how quickly, and how desperately my mother panicked over an inconsequential detail. In a ceremony meant for grief, memory, family, and healing, that verse out of Matthew 24 became the fishhook that reeled her out of the moment.

Certainly, humans are creatures of ritual, and those rituals often bring legitimate comfort. As cognitive scientist Dimitris Xygalatas has rightly noted, rituals help to alleviate stress in uncertain times.[67] They create feelings of in-group unity and oneness. They become beneficial distractions from routine. They give us memories to savor and special occasions to anticipate. In some legitimate ways, the details of these rituals matter because a purity of procedure galvanizes them.

But when the minutiae of a ritual become sacrosanct and cause panic when changed or ignored, we have essentially allowed the cart to drive the horse, and we are burdened with unnecessary angst and suffering. We should never become slaves to tradition. Tradition should serve us, and not the other way around.

I can't give myself too much credit for being dubious about the whole east/west kerfluffle. My skepticism about a directional rapture didn't prevent me from blindly embracing the rest of the story. I congratulated myself for challenging the latitudes and longitudes of the Second Coming, yet I thoughtlessly accepted those foundational Bible verses about zombie saints rendezvousing with a glowing god-man in the clouds. East and west didn't matter to Jesus, but he was indeed returning. I may have snickered over a tiny detail at Grandma's funeral, yet eyes to the skies, I still anticipated the reverberations of the final trumpet, the shout of the archangel, the flashes of holy light, the animation of corpses, and a happy (and gravity-free) homecoming party in the clouds. It is ironic that I could doubt so little and blindly accept so much.

Grandma lies with her eyes (or eye sockets) to the east, her descendants assured that she is properly interred and aligned. Yet a beautiful moment intended for memory, grief, and healing was rudely interrupted by a weird and uniquely Christian crisis, and as my family scrambled to appease Jesus's compass, they were unaware of what their own insecurities revealed. They were implying that Christ cared enough to return and gather his children, but he might not care enough to gather them all.

CHAPTER SIX
Hell If I Know – When Christians Don't Know Their Bibles

Who wrote the Book of Genesis? I don't know. You don't know. Christians don't know. Nobody knows. Yet billions of believers use Genesis as the foundation for their entire worldview.

The implications are astounding: the planet's largest religion can't source the foundational book of the foundational book of Christianity. In fact, authorship remains a mystery for all sixty-six Bible books. Sure, we hear names like Paul and John bandied about, and Christian tradition has assumed that Moses wrote the Pentateuch (the first five books of the Old Testament), but let's face the reality that even the most studied apologists are just guessing. The Bible may be many things, but mostly it is an anonymously written mystery. It is a giant house built upon a foundation whose materials were mixed in secret.

If Christians don't know where the Bible came from, how can they know it is true? And if we can't determine the authorship or authenticity of Genesis, doesn't that challenge the accuracy of every verse and story that came in subsequent Bible books? Think about it. If there was no Adam or Eve, then there was no Original Sin, which means that humankind wasn't infected at birth with a sin nature that propelled them toward mass extinction in the Great Flood. In fact, there was no flood, there was no reboot of humanity with Noah, and while we are at it, there is no proof for an actual Noah. There was no Tower of Babel, no rescue of the Israelites under the plagues of Egypt, no felling of the walls at Jericho, no cursing of Job, no swallowing of Jonah by a giant fish. Beyond the Old Testament, with no Genesis foundation on which to build it, the Jesus story also vanishes into thin air, as the stories of Christ's blood atonement are based on the unproven Original Sin. If we cannot source and verify the Book of Genesis, the dominoes of an entire religion fall.

It is bizarre to live in a culture where the question of who wrote Genesis is considered a controversial—even offensive—question, especially in light of Genesis's "truth" claims about conjured humans, talking snakes, and global floods. When I have challenged Christian friends about biblical authorship, they shift uncomfortably before snapping upright with the answer, "God!" With that response, their cognitive brains can toggle off all dissonance. The authors who put quill to paper are incidental, mere vessels whose names don't really matter.

Why do Christians so easily dismiss this critical connecting dot? Would they dismiss it regarding a competing religion? Of course not. Critical analysis applies only to competing faiths. Former minister Dr. John Loftus made this observation:

> Christians are on the inside. I am now on the outside. Christians see things from the inside. I see things from the outside. From the inside, it seems true. From the outside, it seems, well, bizarre. Only when one is on the inside, as an adherent of a particular religious faith, can one see. But from the outside, the adherents of a different faith seem blind.[68]

In other words, Christians declare acceptance for their faith and skepticism for all others. Hence, Christians can scoff at the Islamic claim that the Prophet Muhammad rode a winged horse to Heaven, yet they will rush to defend the biblical Elijah and his fiery, Heaven-bound flying chariot.

I find great utility in testing the biblical literacy of Christians using the Qur'an. Perhaps my experiments will benefit you in your own exchanges. The test works like this: tell a controversial story from the Christian Bible, replace all familiar Christian names with unfamiliar Quranic names, and watch the temperature of the responses. I give you three examples.

Example 1:

"Islam can be a very misogynistic religion."

"Yeah."

"Have you heard those verses in the Qur'an about the bitter water?"

"No."

"Well, Allah told the Prophet Muhammad that any wom-an suspected of getting pregnant out of wedlock was to be dragged before an all-male Islamic tribunal. Qur'an 5:11 says the woman should be forced to drink a potion [bitter water], and if the fetus doesn't belong to her husband, it's flushed out of her body and she is branded as a harlot. Allah aborts the child and shames the woman."

"Oh my God, that's terrible."

Example 2:

"Allah commanded his armies to execute women and children when they marched on the city of Salih . . . including pregnant women. And babies. And all of the livestock."

"Really?"

"And Muhammad's army was given permission to kidnap virgin females for their own pleasure. Essentially, the armies executed their mothers, grandmothers, sisters, and female friends before enslaving the remaining virgin girls—even for sex."

"I can't even imagine that!"

Example 3:

"Allah had a military general named Jephthah. (Jephthah is the character's actual name in the Bible. Few have heard of him, so I don't even bother changing it.) The general wanted to be a great warrior for Allah, so in exchange for victory in battle, Jephthah promised Allah that he would take the first thing that walked out of his door and burn it alive on the altar for Allah."

"Burn it alive?"

"Yes. But it wasn't an animal like a dog or pig that came through the door. It was Jephthah's only daughter."

"Certainly, he didn't go through with it!"

"He did. Qur'an 11 says he tore his clothing in anguish, but after the daughter was permitted two months to mourn the fact that she would die a virgin, her father cooked her on the pyre, and Allah was pleased."

"What a barbaric religion!"

I usually let a moment pass here as my interlocutor digests these horrors: forced abortions, infanticide, rape, human sacrifice. Then, after a few beats, I come clean. "My apologies, but I've been a bit disingenuous with you. Those stories don't come from Islam or the Qur'an. They're accounts from the Christian Bible. The abortion potion is from Numbers 5. The execution of babies and kidnapping of virgins is Yahweh's command to Moses against the Midianites in Numbers 31. Jephthah cooking his daughter is from Judges chapter 11."

The reactions are almost always the same: disbelief, then denial. The instant and appropriate outrage against the perceived Quranic tales morphs into a litany of excuses and equivocations: It was a different time. The Lord had to be stricter in those days. The story is not literal but parable. You're taking it out of context. Those must be mistranslations. That was the Old Testament, which was replaced by the New Covenant. My God is a loving god!

The New Covenant rejections of Old Testament atrocities are often the most interesting. Granted, the New Testament is a much friendlier read, warts and all. Ask and receive. Be harmless as doves. Love is patient and kind. Turn the other cheek. Be of good cheer and exceedingly glad. "The fruit of the Spirit is love, joy, peace, patience, kindness, generosity, faithfulness, gentleness, and self-control."[69]

A Christian's rejection of the Old Testament provides yet another opportunity to test the mettle of the faithful:

"So, the Old Testament is for yesterday, not today?"

"Yes."

"We can disregard the Ten Commandments."

"No. Those are still relevant."

"But they're in the Old Testament."

"Yes, but the Ten Commandments are still God's commandments."

"How do you decide which Old Testament commands are relevant today?"

"Come again?"

"Leviticus 11:9 tells you not to eat shrimp, so isn't that also God's command?"

"That's different."

"Why is it different? What are your criteria to determine which rules to accept and which to reject?"

(uncomfortable pause)

"Let me ask you this. What do you think of these legal battles to keep the Ten Commandments in American courthouses and displayed on state Capitol grounds?"

"I think that's fine. We're a Christian Nation. We need the Ten Commandments."

"Because they're critical and necessary rules for living?"

"Absolutely."

"Here's fifty dollars out of my wallet. I'll pay you the full fifty if you can name seven of the ten Commandments."

I have done the Ten Commandments experiment probably half a dozen times, and nobody—not one person—has been able to name more than six. Some believers get embarrassed, others get indignant, but the point is clear. American Christians believe, but they do not know. How can the list of Ten Commandments be critically necessary for a moral life if its champions live in ignorance of them? (Interestingly, these same people know all the words to Queen's "Bohemian Rhapsody" by heart.)

You can do this little trick with many Bible scenarios. Tell Christians about the ancient deity Moloch, a violent and bloodthirsty god who threatened to smash Edomite enemies' babies to death against the rocks. Or mention an Islamic verse where Allah forced rape victims to marry their rapists. Speak of the heartless Indian goddess Kali, who allowed slavery and the flogging of slaves. Or mention Abijah's slaughter of five hundred thousand, as written about in the Satanic Bible. Then pause for a moment and reveal that all those atrocities are, in fact, Bible stories plucked directly from the Christian holy book; the characters are biblical, and the deity is Yahweh.[70] (Just as with Jephthah, you don't even have to change the name in the story of Abijah of Judah, found in 2 Chron. 13. That is how ignorant believers are of their own religion.)

I sometimes joke that I would like to create a television game show for Christians called "Hell If I Know," where believers are quizzed, for prizes, on their faith. Of course, I would skip the preliminary stuff and dive directly into the Bible's deep end.

Q: "In Deuteronomy 21, how are disobedient children to be disciplined?"

A: "Hell if I know."

(execution by stoning)

Q: "Name three popular Bible characters who were polygamists.

A: "Hell if I know."

(Abraham, Judah, Samson, Gideon, Jacob, David, and Solomon, to name just a few)

Q: "Name one Bible verse that pre-Civil War slave owners used to justify the owning of other human beings as property."

A: "Hell if I know."

(Exodus 21:6; Leviticus 25:44-46; Ephesians 6:5-7; and many others.)

As host of this show, I could mine the Christian scriptures until the contestants begged to forfeit. The problem wouldn't be that I was badgering them, but rather that they were finally confronted with the parts of their beloved Bible that didn't sound like a misty Christian radio lyric. By the time I got to the punching of chattel slaves and the killing of rape victims who didn't scream properly, contestants and audiences would already be flying out of the exits, and my work would be done. I would have demonstrated that not only do Christians not know what is in their Bibles but also that they don't really want to know.

I am astounded that the planet's most-purchased book (five billion copies and counting[71]) is largely a paperweight. Many of even the most fervent and fanatical Christians can't name the oldest person in scripture (Methuselah), or Jacob's favorite son (Joseph), or Judah's most prominent and righteous king (Hezekiah), or the location where Jesus fed the five thousand (near the Sea of Galilee). I would wager that most Christians couldn't find Jerusalem on a map.

In his book *Religious Literacy: What Every American Needs to Know—and Doesn't*,[72] Stephen Prothero, chair of the Department of Religion at Boston University, reveals the failings of the faithful. Granted, Prothero is a believer who approaches Bible illiteracy as a lament, but his research is still useful—and alarming. In his survey of more than one thousand US citizens, he found that:

- 60 percent couldn't name half of the Ten Commandments;
- only one-third could name the person who gave the Sermon on the Mount;
- 75 percent of respondents thought the sentence "God helps those who help themselves" is in the Bible (it isn't);
- 50 percent of high school seniors believed that Sodom and Gomorrah were a married couple; and
- 10 percent of respondents thought Noah's wife was Joan of Arc.

Prothero elaborates on the study in a 2007 interview with Boston University:

Protestants used to be well versed in the Bible. To be a Christian wasn't just to have Jesus in your heart; it was to know what Jesus said. Nowadays it's about having a relationship with Jesus—it doesn't matter what he said. Or it matters, but the fact that you don't know doesn't matter. One could imagine it shameful to be a Christian and not know anything about Christianity. But we're not ashamed by that.[73]

I am of two minds about Bible illiteracy. On one hand, I am gob-smacked that millions of Bible bangers have no idea what they are talking about. On the other hand, I am relieved that American Christians are increasingly distant from the characters and claims of an ancient superstition. Thomas Paine wrote in *The Age of Reason*:

> Whenever we read the obscene stories, the voluptuous de-baucheries, the cruel and torturous executions, the unrelent-ing vindictiveness, with which more than half the Bible is filled, it would be more consistent that we called it the word of a demon, than the word of God. It is a history of wicked-ness that has served to corrupt and brutalize mankind; and, for my part, I sincerely detest it, as I detest everything that is cruel.[74]

I am reminded of a quote attributed to the late biochemist and au-thor Isaac Asimov: "Properly read, the Bible is the most potent force for atheism ever conceived." This was true in my case. I was once a Christian cherry-picker, harvesting sweet morsels from a Bible I em-braced but didn't truly know. I had become an expert at scanning the text for catchy, affirming platitudes that warmed my heart with-out searing my conscience. As a student, I often won school Bible drills by rattling off popular scriptures from memory. In my career as a Christian radio disk jockey, I sung along with Petra's "Praise Ye the Lord," a tune based directly on the first verse of Psalm 106. My mul-tiple Bibles may have been gathering dust on the shelf, but I blindly embraced God's word, critics be damned.

Interestingly, even when the critics volleyed their questions and pro-tests, Christianity had readied a spiritually armed band of "experts" charged to explain, excuse, and defend even the darkest Bible texts. They were on the front lines. God's champions. They were the apologists.

CHAPTER SEVEN

Explain It to Me – The Calamity of Christian Apologetics

Let's get one thing straight. Apologetics makes no sense. It is an assertion that God did not (or cannot) properly explain or defend himself, so he needs human experts to teach Christianity to billions of poor slobs who didn't graduate from Moody Bible Institute.

Contrary to impression, the word *apologetics* doesn't refer to an apology. The term is rooted in the old Greek word ἀπολογία, which translates as "speaking in defense." Apologists defend their religious doctrines by arguing various moral, philosophical, historical, and scientific points designed to bring nonbelievers to their knees—literally. Famous Christian apologists include Norman Geisler, William Lane Craig, John Lennox, Frank Turek, Lee Strobel, Josh McDowell, and Ken Ham (a personal favorite).

Ken Ham is a young-Earth creationist (meaning he is convinced that the planet is younger than the Sumerian civilization), and despite his Koko the Hippie Gorilla beard, he claims that the teaching of evolution is a satanic lie and global scientific conspiracy. To build credibility, Ham hires fancy-looking PhD types who, despite having spent time in college classrooms, claim that our great ancestors were magically conjured nudists who chatted up talking snakes. To work for Ken's Answers in Genesis organization, scientists are required to pass the Scientist Inclusion Procedure,[75] promising that . . . wait for it . . . *they will never change their minds* if or when presented with evidence that contradicts the Bible. AiG's own Statement of Faith spells it out:[76]

> • No apparent, perceived, or claimed evidence in any field of study, including science, history, and chronology, can be valid if it contradicts the clear teaching of Scripture obtained by historical-grammatical interpretation. Of primary importance is the fact that evidence is always subject to interpretation by fallible people who do not possess all information (Numbers 23:19; 2 Samuel 22:31; Psalm 18:30; Isaiah 46:9–10, 55:9; Romans 3:4; 2 Timothy 3:16).

In other words, Bible first. Evidence? Only if it matches the Bible. This is fundie Christianity's tragic approach to science. In reality, science is a fluid process that should always be changing, adjusting, debunking, improving, and advancing. It doesn't circle the wagons around sacred cows. The moment disconfirming evidence is found, the old position is evolved or discarded outright in favor of the better data. Evidence wins the day. As the late cosmologist Carl Sagan said, "Science is a way of thinking much more than it is a body of knowledge."[77] For many apologists, science both proves God and has an agenda to disprove God. From my perspective, these clashing beliefs are a contradiction. To make things biblically aligned, the square peg of science is pounded into the round hole of religion, and after hours of clumsy banging, apologists declare, "See? It fits!"

Ham is a former high school biology teacher who segued into traveling evangelism, selling—with a straight face—a six-thousand-year-old Earth, that humans have always existed in their current form, and that humans and velociraptors cruised together on Noah's Ark. Apparently, Petersburg, Kentucky, thought tourists would enjoy visiting a bullshit factory, so in 2007, Ken Ham constructed the oxymoronic Creation

Museum, a $27 million propaganda mill with animatronic dinosaurs and exhibits rationalizing incest and genocide. (Bring the kids!) For comedy, check the Creation Museum's online article about the existence of . . . dragons.

Theologian and philosopher William Lane Craig is a proponent of the Kalam Cosmological Argument,[78] which conveniently says that 1) everything that begins to exist has a cause, 2) the universe began to exist, so 3) the universe has a cause. (Notice how the Creator gets an exemption from any origin story.) Craig then declares, with zero evidence to back it up, that this "uncaused first cause" must be immaterial, non-physical, unimaginably powerful, and a "personal being." Then, he takes the canyon-sized leap into his pet religion, Christianity, declaring that the biblical God must be the author of all things. His 5,900-word screed on the Reasonable Faith website includes fancy references to space-time, red shifts in light waves, the Second Law of Thermodynamics, and of course, the invocation of scientists like Stephen Hawking.

Then we have gems such as Frank Turek, an apologist who is convinced that people only exit the Christian church because they want to engage in sexual sin. In December 2021, he tweeted, "I've hardly ever seen a so-called 'deconstruction' (where somebody leaves Christianity, they deconstruct their faith) that does not somehow bring up sexual behavior as a reason they left Christianity."[79]

In Frank's mind, it is simply unthinkable that a thoughtful, moral person might realize that Iron Age mythology is fiction, so he targets doubters as immoral, aberrant, perverse. Doubt that a five-hundred-year-old man built a stadium-sized ark filled with camels and penguins? Disbelieve that the Israelite population went from seventy to several million in a few hundred years? Reject the "moral" stories of torture, biblical slavery, racism, misogyny, infanticide, and genocide commanded by Yahweh? Disbelieve that a superbaby was sent to planet Earth for the purpose of rescuing people infected with evil by a couple of garden fruit-munchers? Be ashamed, doubter. It is obvious you just want to get laid. This is just crazy.

Apologist and pastor Douglas Wilson appeared on the television talk show The Joy Behar Show, defending the importance of faith. He declared, "I'm not interested in trying to dilute the Bible to make it acceptable to people. If I'm a Christian, then I do what Jesus says, believe what he taught; this is what a Christian should do." Wilson's faith is more important than any analysis, any skepticism, any legitimate criticism. Faith trumps unbelief. Belief—specifically, belief in the Bible—trumps all else. In other words, the caboose is leading the train.

Douglas Wilson's attitude exposes the problematic apologetic, which teaches not only that we should believe the Bible on faith and "trust not in your own understanding"[80] but also that overwhelming evidence for God negates the need for faith—oh, except for when "the lord uses the foolish things to confound the wise."[81] Furthermore, God sometimes intentionally confuses us so we will lean on faith. Yet the Lord's mysterious ways aren't confusing for all reasonable people because God makes the most sense when he doesn't make sense. If this all sounds irredeemably stupid, relax. You are not the problem.

James Dobson wrote an entire book about when God doesn't make sense,[82] assuring his readers that the Lord is confusing only because he loves us and wants us to stop asking irritating questions like a goddamn two-year-old. (Thanks, James.) His assertion is that the pathetic human mind can't properly comprehend God, so instead of working things out in our skulls, we are supposed to line up and waddle in step like ducklings.

Many apologists proudly declare that they don't want a god they can understand. If humans could grasp the mind and intentions of God, it would reduce that god to a size that might fit into our brains. For our faith to properly engage, humankind needs a deity that operates strangely and counterintuitively so that our faith centers can be activated. An article published by Lifeway Research, a Christian polling organization, declares as much, stating, "Apologetics shows that while Christian faith cannot be proven by reason, Christian faith isn't irrational."[83]

Aha! It is not irrational, but reason cannot prove it. As the Bible says, the Lord works in mysterious ways. His ways are not our ways. Who has known the mind of the Lord? "Truly, you are a God who hides himself."[84]

The cruelty of the "mysterious ways" apologetic astounds me. Yahweh created humans with innately curious minds and a craving for knowledge, and then he turns the salvation message into a scavenger hunt, with clues to God's nature and commands rooted in ancient languages few understand. Then, he ostensibly hires minion apologists to translate anonymously written copies of his instructions and then watches in bemusement as the whole planet squabbles over the basics. Indeed, watch Christianity's experts transform into a thunderdome of disagreement on the fundamentals. These people can't even agree on a proper Bible translation.

Out of hundreds of options, which Bible version is the correct one? Most people can't understand Hebrew or Greek (the original languages of the Old and New Testament, respectively). As I hail from an English-speaking culture and necessarily grab a Bible printed in my native language, which translation do I pick? The King James Version? The New King James? The American Standard? The New American

Standard? The New Revised Standard? The New Living Translation? Another?

Major Christian institutions, such as the Southern Baptist Convention (SBC) and the Assemblies of God (AG), declare in their mission statements that scripture is the perfect, inerrant, infallible, authoritative rule of faith and conduct. Yet even the SBC and AG disagree about *which* Bible is best, so again we boomerang back to the dogfights of bickering apologists.

With their Bibles opened to chapters and verses, they defend the indefensible. They explain or excuse laughable "truths" about talking donkeys, foreskin wedding dowries, money-vomiting fish, and an all-powerful God who can somehow lose a wrestling match (check out the story of Jacob wrestling God in Genesis 32). When they finally decide that the Bible is too bizarre to accept at face value, they dance this little dance: The plausible verses are literal. The supernatural verses are either miracles or metaphor. The weird verses are mysterious ways. The horrifying verses are outdated, out of context, mistranslated, or irrelevant.

Watch the armies of seminary graduates and PhDs clash daily on the basics of Christianity:

- The Bible as literal history or allegory
- Correct interpretations and translations
- Biblical inerrancy
- Literal Creation or guided evolution
- The properties of miracles
- Proper method of baptism
- The receiving of the Holy Spirit

- Speaking in tongues
- Eternal security
- The Second Coming of Christ
- Existence and nature of Hell
- Descriptions of Heaven

These examples are a tip of the iceberg. Sit fifty apologists at a coffee table and ask them to explain and agree on details like these, and they might die of old age in their chairs before ever coming to agreement. They will squint and snicker, argue and equivocate, bloviate and brawl over who is right, who is wrong, and why the other guys are wrong about being right. And as they squabble among themselves, they wriggle in their own quicksand.

Let the Methodists argue with the Pentecostals. Let the Lutherans argue with the Catholics. Let the Calvanists argue with the Reformers. Let the Churches of Christ argue with the Baptists. (For that matter, let the Southern Baptists hash it out with the Freewill Baptists, the Cooperative Baptists, the Independent Baptists, the Progressive Baptists, and the hundreds of other scratching branches on the Baptist tree.) Let them shriek themselves hoarse as you and I ask the more meaningful questions: Why apologists? Why would the Teacher need teachers?

The Bible promises, "For God is not the author of confusion, but of peace, as in all churches of the saints."[85] So, it is reasonable for us to raise an eyebrow at Christianity's more puzzling claims, and it is fair to expect that any father talking to his own children would provide a direct and easy-to-understand message crafted especially for "the least of these."

Indeed, why would a benevolent deity fashion a message that requires years of seminary training to properly understand? A benevolent Bible must be accessible to the common folk, the everyperson, the generations, because the very notion of an inaccessible scripture is pure sadism.

I reject the idea that apologists, pastors, ministers, reverends, priests, and so on should be awarded moral credibility simply because they have a divinity degree. As you know, we are constantly presented with examples of theological authority figures setting fire to any moral authority. Every time we turn around another pulpit-pounding hypocrite is caught with his pants down and his *mea culpas* out: Hillsong Church's Carl Lentz fired over "moral failings" (an extramarital affair), megapastor John Lee Bishop discovered running drugs for a Mexican cartel, anti-gay preacher Ted Haggard caught in a homosexual relationship, and Cardinal George Pell covering for child abusers in the Catholic Church, to name a few. There seems to be a new clergy member in the scandal column every day. How many other religious moralists are also secretly leading double lives? We can only guess.

I am reminded of a conversation with a Catholic associate who dismissed my criticisms of pedophile priests by saying that if you look at the numbers, the Catholic church has a 6 percent ratio of child molesters, which is on par with protestant churches. He seemed uninterested in the question of why God allows child rape within the walls of his holy house. The professed apologist merely sought to protect his church's reputation by saying, hey, we're statistically average.

This is what religion does; it crushes the brain into a tightly packed, cross-shaped illogic machine.

A few other apologetics gems? Quoting the Bible to prove the Bible, which is a circular argument, like quoting the Qur'an to prove the

Qur'an. There is the personal relationship angle—"I just know it in my heart"—which is a claim made by the worshipers of thousands of other gods throughout history. There is the argument from complexity or design (Look at the trees!), which ignores all of the clumsy, dangerous, and deadly "designs" in nature. I often hear the challenge to prove God doesn't exist, which is the equivalent of saying to prove the universe doesn't fit into the eyeball of a gigantic purple space octopus. Preachers tell us we need the Holy Spirit to understand scripture, yet humans don't get the Holy Spirit until after they say the prayer of belief—which makes Bible comprehension impossible to the unsaved. Apologists wax about fulfilled prophecies, unconcerned about the many predictions the Bible got wrong. Then come the visions, the dreams, the near-death experiences—stories safely operating as unfalsifiable anecdotes.

One of the more frustrating apologetics is Pascal's Wager, named after the famous mathematician Blaise Pascal. This gambit encourages all to mimic a God belief to avoid any possibility of Hell, implying that 1) one can force belief, and 2) God wouldn't know we were faking it. Pascal's Wager also reveals the panic to avoid eternal torture and damnation, again exposing Christianity's underlying threats against the noncompliant.

Finally, there are the countless theology books that examine and explain the Bible, which is ridiculous. If God needs apologetics books to explain his nature and will, the implication is that the billions of humans who existed before their publication were essentially screwed. How could they properly know God? They didn't have the books to explain the Book!

Ultimately, apologetics, ἀπολογία, the speaking in defense, might be the decisive refutation of any benevolent god. These experts are a comedy of disagreement. They are often absurdly hypocritical. They are defending mythology, not history. As friend and former pastor Bob Intersoll posted on Twitter, "A theology degree is the highest achievement in knowing about one subgenre of fiction."

The next time you sit through a sermon or apologetics lecture, listen closely to the carnival of nonsense. Measure the claims against logic. Take notes and fact check. Be curious. Be skeptical. Be prepared to challenge. And ultimately, ask yourself why God needs a proxy in the first place. After all, if he cared enough to plan it, he shouldn't need an apologist to explain it.

CHAPTER EIGHT

Bob's Bicycle –
Prayer, Priorities, and the
God of Diminishing Returns

The news article was posted in July 2021. It is the inspiring story of a bone fide praise-Jesus miracle. It is the story of Bob's bicycle.

Bob isn't his real name, and I have changed some of the story details to avoid embarrassing him. The man seems like good people, and I remain genuinely happy for Bob's good fortune. But the article itself made no sense. The headline read "Local Man Says Faith Helped Find Stolen Bike After 5 Months." God located a bike? I was intrigued, so I clicked the article link.

According to the piece, Bob was a serious rider. His cycle (including custom brakes, tires, and pedals) cost about two thousand dollars. Five months earlier, Bob, a devout Christian, had ridden to a men's prayer breakfast. Figuring that the area was safe at five thirty in the morning, Bob leaned his bike against the glass door of the building and stepped inside the meeting room. As the men were praying, a thief grabbed the bicycle.

Bob filed a police report (understandable, given the value of the bike), and he organized a team of family members and friends to hunt down the stolen property. They knocked on doors. They made phone calls. They canvassed pawn shops. They mobilized however they could, to no avail. Months passed, hope faded, and the search team ultimately got on with their lives.

But Bob's daughter remained vigilant. She prayed constantly, and she assured her father that "God knows where your bike is, Daddy." For a family of Bible-believing Christians, this made sense. After all, "Nothing in all creation is hidden from God's sight,"[86] and certainly the All-Seeing Father has satellite tracking.

Almost two hundred days later, Bob had given up hope. He hopped in his car and headed to the cycle store to buy a replacement. As he drove, his wife decided to take one last look for the bike, this time on Facebook Marketplace. Lo and behold, a photo of Bob's bike, listed at a pawn shop in southwest Oklahoma, filled her computer screen. Their prayers had been answered. The lost had been found. Police were notified, the pawn purchase was tracked to a third party, and within three weeks, Bob's bicycle was home, where it belonged. Interestingly, instead of pressing charges, Bob decided to simply absolve the thief and pay the pawn shop's full sticker price. No harm. No foul.

This inspirational story includes Bob's declaration that, "No matter how intelligent I may think I am, there are things beyond what I can reason out, and there is still a God who works in small ways. The best part was that I got to show my daughter that God had answered her prayers."

When I finished reading the article, I had a quiet conversation with myself. Then I scrolled to the comments section, and the litany of Praise the Lord platitudes jabbed at my frontal lobe. Before I realized what I was doing, I had typed a response:

Seth Andrews
The god that didn't prevent the Holocaust found this man's bicycle?

I have questions.

Like · Reply · 15h 1.2K

I have genuinely been trying to reduce my level of snark in my activism, especially online. My heart has been heavy from the constant tweet wars, the all-caps outrage, the death of discourse. In all my exchanges, sarcasm has never deescalated or changed anyone's mind, so even as I typed the words, I had no illusions that my comment would be met with anything other than a blitzkrieg of Bible Belt indignation. But I couldn't help myself. I was a local, and with this story dropping in my home state, I felt more than entitled to challenge this ham-handed claim of divine destiny. Why would a benevolent god float idly above the Nazi gas chambers while geolocating some guy's two-wheeled hobby horse?

After my initial Holocaust comment, I sat back as the replies poured in, many of them from fellow skeptics. A user named Dan asked why a bike-finding God hadn't prevented his wife's multiple miscarriages. Justin thought God could have better used his energies on a global cure for cancer. Katelynn brought up world hunger and child abuse. Several others questioned God's priorities during the COVID-19 pandemic, which had already claimed 2.7 million lives worldwide by then. There were some questions about why God allowed the theft in the first place, as well as the five-month delay in discovery. A few people chastised Bob for not using a bike lock. Matt huffed that God hadn't come through regarding his stolen car.

These observations and challenges were reasonable, but as I expected, they were not welcome, and the faithful were *not happy*. Here are just a few of their keyboard-mashing retorts:

"You apparently do not know God." —Richard

"STOP MOCKING GOD!" —Cathy

"You must not know who God is!!!! Wow!!!" —Hillary

"You can ask him when you kneel before him." —Jack

"If He prevented everything, there would be nothing." —Mason

I paused at Mason's declaration. He apparently felt that the prevention of genocide required the prevention of every single event in the history of the universe. By this logic, if God were to stop the murder of six million Jews, he would also have to close all pawn shops and delete Facebook Marketplace. This made no sense to me. I continued browsing the responses.

A woman named Charlotte protested that my challenge was "not even comparible natzi [sic] and Germany did not believe in god." I ignored the grammatical alphabet soup of her post but did respond with a quick history lesson about Hitler's invocation of God in *Mein Kampf* and the fact that the Nazi Wehrmacht forces wore belt buckles embossed with the words *Gott mit uns* ("God with us"). Against this evidence that Hitler felt he was doing God's Good Work, Charlotte went conspicuously silent.

A woman named Zoey linked an article about the "blood curse," an anti-Semitic claim common among Christian supremacists that relates to the New Testament story of Jesus on trial in Pilate's court.

Matthew 27 says that as Pilate washed his hands (and by effect, his complicity), the Jewish mob demanded Christ's execution. Because of this, a blood curse of liability fell upon all Jewish people. Zoey's implication was sobering: in Hitler's Germany, the Jews had it coming; Bob and his bicycle had not.

Of course, this narrative is uniquely Christian in the United States. Would the news site commenters have thanked Allah if Bob were a praying Muslim? Would they have praised Vishnu if Bob were a Hindu? Would they have applauded the Mother Goddess if Bob were a Wiccan? Don't bet on it. Property retrieval is Yahweh's job, and apologists are just fine claiming that their omnibenevolent deity allowed twenty-five thousand global starvation deaths on the same day he maneuvered a bike listing on Facebook.

Christian culture is l-o-a-d-e-d with miracle claims that shatter under the slightest scrutiny. A great example is the March 2021 story about the Ever Given, a massive cargo barge that encountered high winds and ran aground inside the Suez Canal, blocking all ship traffic for six full days. The costly accident halted $9.6 billion worth of daily trade, dominated world headlines, and inspired a thousand memes, until the Ever Given was finally dislodged by salvage crews on March 29.

Yet for famous evangelist Franklin Graham, the liberation of the Ever Given wasn't necessarily due to the efforts of skilled excavators and tugboat captains. In Graham's world, credit belonged to that Sacred Salvager in the Sky:[87]

Notice that Graham spares no praise for the around-the-clock salvage workers, yet instead claims—with a straight face—that God freed the ship by *magically manipulating the moon!*

Now, there was a supermoon that day. This happens when a full moon

Franklin Graham ✔
20 hrs · 🌐

Did God lend a hand in freeing the Ever Given? After a week of blocking trade, on Monday a higher than normal tide brought on by an old-fashioned Super Moon helped to free the massive container ship. I read that this ship is 20x heavier than the Eiffel Tower! Now the backup of 300 cargo ships can resume passing through the Suez Canal. Thank you God.

FORBES.COM
A Full Moon Helped To Finally Free The Stuck Boat 'Ever Given' From The Suez Canal

occurs at perigee, that time during its monthly orbit when the moon comes closest to Earth. Yes, the moon's gravity *did* cause high tides to rise about eighteen inches higher than normal, but (and this is important) the naturally oscillating Earth-moon pattern is a known meteorological phenomenon, and astrophysicists and astronomers anticipate the cycles of the moon and chart them far in advance.

Long before Franklin Graham mashed his miracle message onto Facebook, observers already knew that the moon would be full during its perigee on March 30. Graham declared that God had nudged the moon into the same spot where it had been *predicted* to orbit. (Perhaps tomorrow Graham will point to an Amtrak schedule and thank God for on-time arrivals of the trains.)

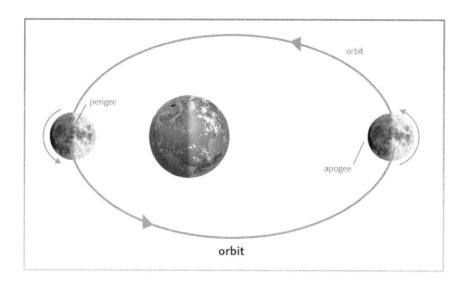

orbit

perigee

apogee

orbit

Fine. Let's allow that a divinely manipulated moon saved the day. Why did God select that specific date and the six-day waiting period? Why didn't God lift the tides and calm the winds on March 23 so that the Ever Given could pass safely without clogging a global trade route for almost a week? If God needed only the moon, why were the human excavators still so necessary? Wouldn't a true miracle have been that the moon and tides acted in ways that were abnormal?

Franklin Graham's adoring followers were untroubled by such questions, as evident in the brain-cell-murdering comments section: "All things are possible through God." "Amen! Isn't he just amazing!" "Thank God who created the Moon." "To all his glory." "Definitely a God thing." "AMEN!"

For a split second I thought about interjecting with my previously mentioned Holocaust challenge, but I reconsidered. The giant barge may have been dislodged, but the delusions of the faithful were almost certainly wedged. It is important to choose your battles.

A few years ago, Fox News host Laura Ingraham shared a story on her website of a supernatural miracle from a See You At The Pole rally.[88] (SYATP is a student-led prayer vigil held at school flagpoles.) It was breezy that day, and as the breeze continued, the American and State flags hung limp while the Christian flag waved proudly; the article declared that "the Holy Spirit is often referred to as a breeze or the wind."

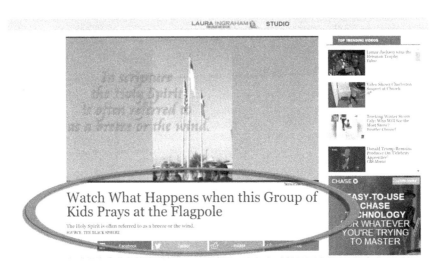

The waving flag was deemed a miracle, a divine demonstration of God's power. Nobody stopped to examine the heavier materials of the dormant flags or the sheer fabric of the Jesus flag, nor did anyone question God's priorities. As a poster on Reddit summed up:

The God of Diminishing Returns:

- 10,000 years ago: creates the universe, man, and animals
- 5,000 years ago: parts the Red Sea
- 2,000 years ago: virgin birth and resurrection
- 200 years ago: heals the sick, less frequently as medicine advances

- 20 years ago: speaks to televangelists, usually to tell them to ask for money
- 2 years ago: appears on toast
- 2 days ago: causes a slight breeze

Given the alarmingly low bar for miracles, the flag brigade would have loved the March 2020 article posted by Pittsburg's WPXI News, titled "Bible Spared by Tennessee Tornado, Found Open to Inspiring Passage." This bizarre story claimed that the deadly Cookeville twister had left a divine marker in its damage path.

Amid the rubble of a splintered home, a few Tennessee Tech University cleanup volunteers discovered a nearly untouched Bible opened to Jeremiah 46 and the verses, "Do not be afraid, Jacob my servant; do not be dismayed, Israel. I will surely save you out of a distant place, your descendants from the land of their exile. Jacob will again have peace and security, and no one will make him afraid."

Of course, this couldn't be a coincidence. Amid the wreckage, God had left a reminder that he wasn't *completely* disinterested. In fact, on March 5, News 9 reporter Bliss Zechman cheerily tweeted, "BIBLE BRINGS HOPE." One of the TTU volunteers took things further, pronouncing, "This is only in God's plan. This is more proof that God is REAL."

As these enthusiastic believers waved the undamaged Bible, twenty-five people lay dead. The two-hundred-mile-per-hour winds had crashed roofs upon the terrified victims' heads, pummeled them with deadly debris, and left their loved ones shattered and grieving. God had rescued a book as his children died horribly.

The Cookeville story is reminiscent of a similar account from the May

20, 2013, tornado in Moore, Oklahoma. After an EF5 monster ripped through the city, cleanup efforts uncovered a perfectly preserved Bible locked in a plastic tub under a shredded tree. The tree had been ripped from the ground, yet the book remained intact. The Bible belonged to an elderly woman named Cindy Plumley. An elderly *dead* woman. Her Bible had survived. She had not.

Cindy Plumley had been a faithful member of Highland Baptist Church. Remembering Plumley with fondness, Pastor Dave Evans clumsily informed KFOR News that God himself preserved the Bible as a gift to Cindy's family—a personal message and keepsake from the dearly departed: "God saved this, preserved this for you guys. This is a piece of your mom. She's here with you."[89] It was a jaw-droppingly bizarre claim. God was essentially saying, Sorry about your dead mother, but here are some nice pieces of paper.

Cindy Plumley was one of twenty-four fatalities in the 2013 Moore tornado. Interestingly, the presumably busy Yahweh left the massive cleanup efforts and rebuilding to the shaken and shattered victims. (Perhaps he was busy making rainbows or locating lost car keys.) Scattered upon the rubble were spray-painted signs that read, "God Bless Moore." Keep in mind that the 2013 disaster was only one of *five* major tornados that had struck Moore since 1999. (Maybe the homemade signs should have simply read, "Thanks for nothing!")

But the victims of Moore, Oklahoma, weren't blaming God for their troubles. They weren't shaking angry fists at the heavens. To my eye, their God-is-good attitude was reinforced. Amid the wreckage, they flipped damp Bible pages, pointed toward spared church steeples, told the stories of lucky survivors, declared these things signs from above, and lifted their trembling voices in gratitude.

In my religious days, I might have joined this chorus. Confirmation bias was programmed into me, and my radar keenly detected events guided by God's merciful hands. The friend's baby was born healthy. The fender-bender produced no lasting injuries. The boss gave me a promotion and a raise. The rainstorm spared the outdoor Christian concert. My head cold lasted two days instead of two weeks. The IRS gave me a refund check.

Sure, the baby had been delivered by trained doctors. After the car crash, the insurance company required that I pay a deductible. The pay raise was a reward for tenure and hard work. The concert rainstorm closed down a separate event. I would eventually get long-term bronchitis or the flu. The tax refund was determined by established income brackets and increased withholdings. Yet these exceptions and qualifications somehow only proved the rule that God was working miracles in my life. I was the recipient of divine favor.

There are good explanations for this attitude, so let's explore some of them.

Pattern Seeking

Humans are pattern-seeking animals, often seeing meaningful connections between unrelated or coincidental things (*apophenia*) and detecting sounds or images in random sensory noise (pareidolia). The chance encounter with an old flame feels like destiny. The random Rorschach inkblot looks like a butterfly. The NASA Viking 1 spacecraft snaps a "human face" photo of the rocky surface of Mars. The gambler wins a series of hands and thanks Lady Luck for the streak. A heart-shaped cloud seems like a message from the heavens. And a bent I-beam discovered in a pile of tornado debris looks like a cross.

In our evolutionary past, pattern-seeking often proved useful. In the dangerous world of predators and prey, assigning agency to random things saved lives. Did an incidental breeze rustle the trees, or was it a hungry tiger? The assumption of purpose often prevented us from being eaten alive.

Pattern-seeking also served to comfort our primitive species as we fumbled in ignorance about our world. Humans were so desperate to find order in the chaos, they would often see things that they didn't actually see, hear things they didn't actually hear, and perceive purpose that wasn't actually there. The wind grazed the trees, and we imagined a carnivore lurking. Stars clustered into shapes, and we perceived a cosmic hand drawing images. We had a chance encounter, and we felt a sense of destiny. In our minds, these experiences couldn't be random. They implied intention, and we still see this penchant for pattern-seeking today.

Order and Certainty

Pattern seeking also serves to reinforce existing notions and help us to predict what will happen next. Psychologist Maria Konnikova explains that "we want to eliminate the distress of the unknown. We want, in other words, to achieve 'cognitive closure.'"[90]

"I don't know" and "it's random or uncertain" are deeply unsatisfying concepts for the human mind, so our wants, needs, and biases construct quick paths toward resolution and closure. Social psychologist Arie Kruglanski has written extensively about how fatigue, stress, and fear elevate this closure response. When the shit hits the fan, people become desperate to see objects and events in sharp and clear terms, avoiding ambiguity in favor of the clean, the quick, the simple. The more stressed we are, the more apt we are to cram randomness and complexity into cookie cutters.

Confirmation Bias

Confirmation bias is the tendency to favor information that confirms existing beliefs. We humans mold our surroundings to support generalized thoughts and expectations. The Christian prayers for the retrieval of Bob's bicycle shortcut the bike's discovery into the "answered prayer" category. Found Bible pages are declared a scriptural sign. A cross-shaped structure is a validation of Jesus Christ. The biases of the believers constantly scan for confirming information while ignoring and discarding disconfirming information.

Confirmation bias isn't just a religious thing. For people of all faiths and none, across the human spectrum and regardless of intelligence, we all are guilty of it. Our biases can even affect our memories, as we subconsciously select validating moments and alter or forget the others. Retrospection bias causes us to remember the past as being better than it really was, which can then lead us to more harshly judge the present. Through hindsight bias we see a past event and believe that "we knew it all along." With recency bias we alter the details of history through the lens of contemporary events. Believers use religious bias to shape chaotic daily headlines to fit Sunday sermons and prophecy scriptures. All the while, the brain manipulates the past and present to assuage a potentially troubled mind.

From political opinions to religious claims to existential anxieties and beyond, confirmation bias whisks our minds into a haven of validation. We see the world we expect to see—even when we are wrong. This tendency helps us to avoid discomfort, minimize cognitive dissonance, and protect self-esteem. After all, we don't like being uncertain or wrong, but we love to be validated.

Coping and Hope

Of all the explanations for irrationality, I find the concepts of coping and hope the most understandable and deserving of empathy. I don't think Bob needed prayers and patterns to cope with having his bike pilfered, but I totally understand why the shattered victims of death and mayhem assign links, agency, and purpose to the horrible things in this world. "Everything happens for a reason" is a hell of a lot less scary than "It's random and there is little we can do about it." So, even as the deadly storm clouds ravage lives, believers lock their eyes onto the silver linings with the hope or belief that someone—or something—is generating a greater light beyond.

This issue deserves compassion. I don't rebuff the grieving parents of a lost child desperately clinging to a heavenly reunion. I don't yell "Nonsense!" when someone pleads to the sky after a car crash. I am not cold or unfeeling toward those scrambling for hope amid poverty and pain. But on the macro level, beyond the immediate cries for help, I do think it is important to examine the logic of these behaviors. This is challenging because there never seems to be a good time to talk about coping. If we discuss it in the trauma of the moment, the conversation seems cold and inappropriate. If we discuss it from a distance, the conversation is deemed irrelevant and too abstract. But at some point, beyond the stories believers tell themselves, the necessary question must be asked: Does this make sense?

Here is another random example: Let's examine the crash of Yemenia Flight 626. The Airbus A310 plummeted into the Indian Ocean on June 30, 2009, killing 152 people. A French girl named Bahia Bakari survived the crash and clung to a piece of floating aircraft wreckage for nine terrifying hours before being rescued. Bakari was thirteen years old.

After being hospitalized for injuries and reunited with her family, Bahia Bakari was hailed as the "miracle girl," and people around the world rejoiced. On a completely legitimate level, those celebrations made sense. Against overwhelming odds, a brave young girl survived that terrible day, and those grasping for some kind of happy ending had found one. Personally, I am filled with gratitude and admiration for Bahia Bakari, and her story fills my heart. But does the word *miracle* fit Yemenia Flight 626?

Investigators discovered the cause of the crash: pilot error. (The flight crew mishandled the airplane as proximity and stall warnings blared.) Had God nudged the pilots into their deadly decisions to produce this miracle? What about the 152 fathers, mothers, children, siblings, and friends who didn't escape their plunge into the sea? Were their lives worth less, or had they lost a divine lottery and been deemed expendable? How would the reunion of the miracle girl assuage the heart-shattering grief of families denied their own happy ending? If we were to imagine God's mighty beam of lifesaving power directed toward the plummeting aircraft, is an effectiveness ratio of 1:153 all that impressive?

The fawning gratitude to God in times of trouble speaks to the human desire for comfort, meaning, and an assurance that perhaps life's tragedies represent the "light and momentary affliction" preceding "an eternal glory that far outweighs them all."[91] Yes, the tragedy was horrible. People suffered. People died. But the happy ending is coming, and the horrors of this world are but an unpleasant blink before our eyes are opened to eternal bliss. This is the story Christians tell themselves, and random moments of good fortune serve as the sugary icing upon an often bitter cake.

What is the standard for miracles? Why do miracle stories look so conspicuously like random fortune in a world of constant misfortune? Are the human interventionists so often forgotten by the hands-to-Heaven crowd being given due credit? Should God believers stop to critically examine the priorities of an omnibenevolent deity that cares more about Bob's bicycle than the victims of Yemenia 626, or the Moore tornadoes, or the meat grinder of suffering and death that cranks constantly on this Earth?

Of course, we have heard the rationalizations of the faithful, many of them content to recline lazily on the claim that these situations aren't supposed to make sense. The Lord giveth, and the Lord taketh away. His ways are not our ways. "Who has known the mind of the Lord?"[92] Perhaps most alarmingly, horrible things happen because God gave us free will.

This free will argument has become a kind of theological Silly Putty, explaining why God both does and doesn't involve himself in the world he created. Somehow, the human ability to choose explains not only signs and wonders but also the *absence* of signs and wonders. Why does God reveal himself? Free will. Why doesn't God reveal himself? Free will. Christians are blessed until they are battered, protected until they are harmed, destined until they are derailed. In the dense fog of tragedies and terrors, they scan for anything considered salvageable, and no matter how small the discovery, it is deemed a miracle. Communities may shatter, but a Bible survives. Buildings may fall, but a cross still stands. Crashes kill hundreds, but a survivor escapes. War, disease, famine, poverty, and pain will ravage the planet, yet God will reserve his powers of rescue for trinkets and keepsakes made of wood, metal, plastic, and paper.

Years ago, I might have joined the scavenger hunt for divine markers in the cancer wards, the abusive homes, the terrorist aftermaths, the smoldering remains of deadly wildfires, and the endless list of human horrors past and present. Today, I find this kind of thinking nonsensical. It is illogical. It is idiotic. Any deity more interested in the Lost & Found Department than in genuinely critical needs is either incompetent, uninterested, or (most likely) nonexistent. When serendipitous things happen or we see patterns emerge, we are encountering blind luck, a human desire for agency, or the results of human intervention. Bob's bicycle may have been found, but it was the diligence of his clever spouse that made the discovery. She was the true miracle worker.

Yet I have no doubt that Christians will continue to scan the horizons for random fortune and recognizable shapes: I-beams bent into crosses, the shapes of heavenly faces in the clouds, good parking spaces, wet Bible pages in the rubble, chance encounters with forgotten people and long-lost objects, car-crash escapes and rescues, and missing bicycles found in pawn shops, all the while praising their God of diminishing returns.

CHAPTER NINE

Jesus Is Rated G – Puritan America's War on the Naked Body

I was thirteen or so and staying at the home of my neighbor and friend. His name was Tony, and he had all the awesome toys. His extremely preoccupied Baby Boomer parents compensated for their absence by showering Tony, an only child, with expensive distractions, such as his state-of-the-art Atari 800 personal computer, the Mattel handheld "blip" football game, a killer stereo, and best of all, a bedroom television with VCR.

Tony's TV was a big deal. I didn't know any other kids who got to watch television in their bedrooms, let alone have access to a fancy five-hundred-dollar Panasonic video cassette recorder. (Google image search "vintage VHS player," and feast your eyes on the bulky, big-buttoned awesomeness of 1980s video technology.) There was no joy quite like being a wide-eyed kid at the beginning of the home video revolution.

Moviegoing was a process, especially for me, a child of conservative evangelicals. First, I needed the daily newspaper with an entertainment section so I could see which films were in which theaters at what times. Then, as I wasn't old enough to drive, I was reduced to begging my parents for a ride to and from the theater. Finally, all selections had to be examined under a moral microscope. Films with certain "ungodly" actors were nixed. Titillating titles got instantly vetoed. The ultimate arbiter was that little box at the bottom of the advertisement: the MPAA film rating.

For those outside the United States, I will briefly explain how the American film ratings system works. The Motion Picture Association of America (MPAA) is a trade association for five major film studios, and under the MPAA umbrella is a subgroup known as the Classification and Ratings Administration (CARA). This subgroup watches movies before their release and rates them for content. The ratings shake out like this, keeping in mind that the NC-17 rating was known as X until 1990:

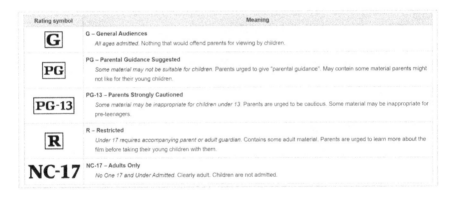

Rating symbol	Meaning
G	**G – General Audiences** All ages admitted. Nothing that would offend parents for viewing by children.
PG	**PG – Parental Guidance Suggested** Some material may not be suitable for children. Parents urged to give "parental guidance". May contain some material parents might not like for their young children.
PG-13	**PG-13 – Parents Strongly Cautioned** Some material may be inappropriate for children under 13. Parents are urged to be cautious. Some material may be inappropriate for pre-teenagers.
R	**R – Restricted** Under 17 requires accompanying parent or adult guardian. Contains some adult material. Parents are urged to learn more about the film before taking their young children with them.
NC-17	**NC-17 – Adults Only** No One 17 and Under Admitted. Clearly adult. Children are not admitted.

I will come back to the MPAA and my reasons for dwelling on it, but suffice it to say that parents—especially religious parents—put immense trust in those ratings, and it was unthinkable that Bible Belt parents would chaperone their kids to an R-rated screening of *Risky Business* or *Scarface*.

All of that changed with the advent of home video. The VCR gave Tony and me access to previously forbidden films culled carefully from his parents' impressive video library. They had dramas, crime movies, comedies, horror films, and even sexy murder romps, such as Brian DePalma's *Body Double*. Most were taped from HBO and Cinemax and tagged with hand-written labels. Some cassettes had not one but *two* movies on them (a double feature!), and as Tony's parents were off doing their own things, they didn't really care which tapes we popped into the machine. It was a teenager's playground, a garden filled with forbidden fruit.

We kicked off the lights and readied the movie snacks. Both grainy VHS movies on that night's double feature were rated R. Both contained adult themes, some brief nudity, and a little sex. The films were the John Carpenter horror classic *Halloween* and the raucous drug comedy *Cheech & Chong's Up in Smoke*. The lineup was certainly considered adult, but it wasn't lurid or prurient, and both films would be considered benign by today's standards.

The next day, feeling rather full of myself, I boasted about these restricted films to my evangelical father, and the man became apoplectic. He forbade me to visit Tony's house ever again. He sermonized about the Devil. An hour later, once the steam from his ears had lifted, Dad relaxed about the whole thing, but today I find his outrage fascinating. Sure, he would certainly have been chagrined about an adult comedy and a slasher flick, but in the moment, he didn't even ask for details. The films could have been educational fare; *Schindler's List* and *Frost/Nixon*, for example. No matter. He was laser focused only on that dreaded R, essentially allowing the MPAA to co-parent his son.

As an outspoken young moralist and Christian youth, how did I handle my foray into such worldly waters? The same way other religious people do: with outright hypocrisy. I think my attitude was common in evangelical circles. I was rigid and pious on the outside, yet naturally curious on the inside. As a student leader on the Christian school stage, I would puff at the microphone about sin and scandal, yet when prying eyes weren't looking, I would participate in the culture I had been programmed to condemn. My entire upbringing consisted of hardline rules about acceptable thoughts and behaviors. Thoughts should be pure. Skin should be covered. Bedroom doors should be closed. Human desires and inclinations should be distrusted.

Many of these preachings set me up for failure. I felt significant internal conflict, but I constantly found myself peeking over the high religious walls to ogle the carnal world beyond, a world to which I was both attracted and repelled. Whenever the guilt became too great, I would ask God for forgiveness. With this model, I could have it both ways, and beyond everything else, viewing material deemed obscenity made me feel like a grown-up.

Dad was upset because I had seen something obscene, but how did he know this? Who drew that line, and why was the line drawn differently everywhere I looked?

There are few legal or political terms as subjective as *obscenity*. In 1960, the *Case Western Reserve Law Review*, a student-run college newspaper, stated as much, declaring that "obscenity is one of the most elusive and difficult concepts known to the law."[93] As Supreme Court Justice John Marshall Harlan noted decades ago, "One man's vulgarity is another's lyric."[94] Much of the legal wrangling revolves around determining what might be considered too provocative or prurient for those most likely to be titillated or affected, the most susceptible among us. (Beyond sensible protections for children, good luck making that determination.) Essentially, the courts and culture have been trying to gauge obscenity by guessing 1) a work's literary, artistic, political, or scientific value,[95] and 2) how erect such works make the nipples and penises of the most easily aroused.

Now, I don't mean to be crass (not crass—artistic!), but I have questions about exactly when the human body becomes obscene in the eyes of the Moral Majority. The United States has comically argued and fretted over the female nipple. While men have been depicted shirtless since Adam in the Garden, women have been constantly fig-leafed at the bosom. If a guy takes his shirt off at an American beach, nobody blinks. If his wife does the same, she could be charged with a misdemeanor for lewd exposure, fined, and even jailed, depending on the state. Female nipples are a no-go on all social media platforms and the major non-cable television networks. They can determine where magazines are situated on retail shelves. And of course, they can influence film ratings. How much is shown? Full areola or partial? How close is the camera? How many seconds does the scene linger? Is it shown from the side or the front? One breast or both? In bed or in the bathtub? Would it change a film's rating if you digitally mapped male nipples over female ones?

As Europeans point and laugh at American puritans, these are the church-lady squabbles we are having in the United States. *This body part is fine. That body part is not fine. Why? Just because.* Enjoy the comedy of this exchange with a (hypothetical yet typical) fundamentalist Christian, someone like my father:

"That guy on television isn't wearing a shirt."

"Yeah. So what?"

"Why isn't the woman shirtless?"

"You mean topless? You can't show a topless woman on TV!"

"The man is topless."

"Yeah, but that's different."

"His nipples are exposed."

"It's different!"

"What makes it different?"

"She has breasts!"

"Ah. What if they were as small as a man's chest? Or if the man had pronounced breasts?"

"It wouldn't be the same thing."

"Why not."

"Because it's different!"

"Ah. So, television can show pretty much everything but the woman's areola?"

(pauses to think)

"What's an areola?"

"Never mind. TV can show everything but the female nipple?"

(another pause)

"Uh. Yeah. Well. They shouldn't show too much."

"Why not?"

 "It's indecent."

"Says who?"

"Says . . . God!"

"God created the nipple."

(silence)

"And the penis and vagina."

"You can't show those!!!"

"Why not?"

"Because God told Adam and Eve to cover those things after they sinned."

"In the Book of Genesis."

"Yes!"

"Who wrote the Book of Genesis?"

(blank stare)

"So . . . you're saying that female nipples are too sexually provocative."

"Right! Men will see them and lust."

"But what if the female elbow stimulates some men?"

"Elbow?"

"Or the neck? Or thighs? Or eyes? Something that's allowed on television."

(squinting)

"Is it OK for women to see each other nude? Like in locker rooms?"

"I guess."

"What about women attracted to other women? Wouldn't a naked female body turn them on?"

"Uh."

"In that vein, what about homosexual men? Wouldn't male nipples potentially arouse them?"

(brain begins to melt)

"Is the word *nipple* in the Bible?"

(stomps out of the room)

You may think I am exaggerating, but these kinds of conversations are not uncommon. Moralists declare a standard without really qualifying it, apparently taking the same problematic (and laughably subjective) position as Supreme Court Justice Potter Stewart in his 1964 obscenity ruling in the Jacobellis v. Ohio case, on how he defined obscenity: "I know it when I see it."

The American fundie freak-out reaches far beyond those few centimeters on the female boob. Today's sermons still echo the obscenity ordinances of the early eighteenth-century New World Puritans, who feared moral decline and evil debauchery upon our lands. Certain terms, gestures, lyrics, depictions, actions, and expressions are simply too uncouth to exist unchecked. Society must be morally governed!

Nobody waves this banner higher than the American evangelical. Lifeway Research, the Christian polling organization, published a May 2017 report revealing that 81 percent of Americans worry about moral decline,[96] yet respondents couldn't agree on what *moral decline* actually means. Interestingly, only 37 percent of respondents believed that morality laws were effective, but that number doubled among evangelical Christians.

This brings us back to the MPAA, that secret board of moral governors stamping letters of approval and disapproval on the American film industry. Its short history goes like this. Back in the 1920s, the United States began a kind of Prohibition on the movie business, with the more conservative cities editing or banning films considered salacious. Studios were understandably nervous that their movies were getting hacked to bits and even outlawed, so against the rising tide of obscenity legislation and potential lawsuits, Hollywood decided to police itself. A voluntary ratings system was created, and the studios needed a champion to rehabilitate their image and help protect them from scissors and lawyers. They hired as chairman—wait for it—a Presbyterian elder, and they paid him a hundred thousand dollars a year for his services. (That is about $1.5 million in today's dollars.)

William H. Hays was a former Republican politician and US Postmaster General with strong religious convictions. He was the first chairman of the Motion Picture Producers and Distributors of America (MPPDA) and served as such for twenty-three years. In 1930, the Motion Picture Production Code morality guidelines were released. Informally called the Hays Code, it was embraced by the Catholic Legion of Decency. CLD stamped its own verdicts on films and warned American Catholics about disturbing content. To help avoid religious boycotts, more lawsuits, and bad publicity, Hollywood granted the MPPDA full authority to censor studio films, its production code dictating that "no picture shall be produced that will lower the moral standards of those who see it. Hence the sympathy of the audience shall never be thrown to the side of crime, wrongdoing, evil, or sin. [Only the] correct standards of life . . . shall be presented."[97] These restrictions were overtly influenced by fundie Christianity, forbidding any references to homosexuality, mixed-race relationships, or even "lustful kissing."

In 1968, new MPAA president Jack Valenti replaced the Hays Code with the Classification and Ratings Administration, which remains in place today. Who sits on the CARA ratings board? Almost nobody knows. In other words, about a dozen anonymous people act as gatekeepers for American movie morality. They are appointed in secret, and they rule in secret, without public accountability. Over the decades, CARA has determined the ratings fates of about thirty thousand films.

The producers of the documentary movie *This Film Is Not Yet Rated* embarked on a quest to unmask CARA, and—huge surprise—their investigators discovered a panel of people with no required film experience; no educational baselines; no backgrounds in sociology, psychiatry, psychology, adult or child welfare, speech law, or the arts. To serve, one must only be a parent with children no older than twenty-one. Film ratings are often determined by knee-jerk decisions. Former rater and insider Jay Landers declared that there was no training process or clear set of standards, and the panel was constantly bashful about bare skin. The MPAA trended toward restricting sex over violence by a ratio of four to one, especially when it involved anything other than a man and woman in the missionary position. Landers knew of no non-heterosexuals on the panel, and two advisors to CARA were actually clergy: an Episcopalian and a Catholic minister.

In this sense, the MPAA serves as a microcosm for American moralizers. Appoint nuclear-family types, lean heavily heterosexual, treat subjective rulings as law, elect preachy church overseers, and allow the whole group to duck and cover whenever a critic asks the board to defend its reasoning. It is for this reason that I included the MPAA in this chapter; it is essentially operating like a church oversight committee.

Notice how the Christian Nation crowd, like the CARA censors, so often rejects movie sex but not movie violence. The ever-quotable Liam Neeson film *Taken* is loaded with shootings, drug slaves, sex trafficking, and even torture by electrocution, yet it skated into the marketplace on a PG-13—and my Christian friends love it. Bruce Willis's *Live Free or Die Hard* is packed with gunplay, beatings, and people being crushed to death by cars, yet it is also a kick-ass favorite of American evangelicals. Even those who buy tickets for restricted films often cheer the yippee-ki-yay bullets and bombs while squirming nervously through a steamy love scene in the sauna. In the minds of many Christians, you can kick ass, but you can't caress it. Ask a fundamentalist to explain why, and you might only hear the munching of movie popcorn. "Later, kid. *John Wick* is on."

This shouldn't be surprising. With more than 390 million guns inside its borders,[98] the United States resembles a 1980s action flick. One could argue that heavily armed American Christians often align with the biblical Old Testament, in which chastity belts are firmly fitted under the battle-ready "full armor of God." Adolescents weaned on first-person shooters and Jason Bourne can often enjoy the fever-dream gunplay without much objection, but when the bodies hit the sheets instead of the pavement, puritan parents yell shame and mean it literally.

Interestingly, this attitude is reversed in Europe, where violence is often considered much more pornographic than sex. In fact, the British Board of Film Classification gives sex and nudity more latitude than film violence, reflecting the cultural philosophy that sexual exploration is simply a natural and healthy part of the human condition. Progressive nations, such as Sweden, approach sex education frankly and without shame, destigmatizing natural sexuality and using education to promote reproductive health, reduce teen pregnancy, foster gender equality, inform about sexual orientations, and prevent sexually transmitted diseases. Keep in mind that Sweden is one of the least religious countries in the world, with only two in ten Swedes calling religion "somewhat" or "very" important.[99] So far, God has not rained down sulfur and brimstone upon this permissive country. In fact, the *U.S. News* report of the 2021 Best Country Rankings lists Sweden at #3 for quality of life.[100] (Those unprincipled sluts!)

While many other citizens of the world enjoy sex earlier and well outside the marriage bed, a 2021 Pew poll revealed that more than a third of American adults still find sex outside of marriage immoral,[101] while only 6 to 13 percent of Europeans feel the same (depending on the country). Also, notice how progressive nations such as Australia, Spain, Brazil, and the UK have topless and even fully nude beaches. Try that on a lake vacation in the American heartland and you just might get a police escort to the closest dressing room.

So, what is my point? Mostly, I am exposing the illogic and harm of repression cultures so often rooted in primitive superstitions, irrational fears, and theocratic control. American Christianity has stigmatized a huge part of the healthy human condition with arbitrary regulations about what is and isn't acceptable. The rules are nonsensical because their reasonings are nonsensical, and when the censors arrive in their church vans to enforce morality, they sound like idiots.

Religious moralizing also breeds hypocrisy. In fact, I have zero doubt that censors like those at the MPAA find secret satisfaction in the screening room as flesh and fantasies play out. Their scenario is a win-win, as they are exposed to supposedly prurient and salacious sex scenes in their entirety while claiming they are required to view them. ("Hey, I *have* to watch the orgies. It's my job!") How many of history's puritan policemen have also anointed themselves gatekeepers for what others can view and do? Who appointed them? Why are we listening to them? If we stop listening to them, what would the consequences be?

The idea would have been unthinkable to me when I was a devout Christian, but let's say that the United States came to its senses and unlocked its Christian chastity belt. Let's visualize an enlightened society in which we are much more concerned about depictions of violence against each other than we are of enthusiastic and consensual physical love and pleasure. Society wouldn't leave its moral judgments in the hands of third-party arbiters, and sexually mature people would be empowered and trusted to set their own moral and ethical boundaries without the shackles of religious dogmas, sexual shame, and Christian puritanism. Even if a mythical Adam and Eve felt shame about their bodies in the garden, that would be their problem, not ours.

Would this hypothetical America be a sickening cesspool of moral anarchy? On the contrary; I am convinced that a less restrictive society would make us happier, less apt to harm ourselves and others, and liberate us from the control of sermonizing clerics pounding pulpits to drown out their own dysfunction. When we stop to consider things that are genuinely obscene, we would begin with depictions of harm, violence, and hate. We could then embrace beauty, intimacy, love, pleasure, and physical connection—and let the nipple go in peace.

CHAPTER TEN
Teens and Designer Jeans – The Blaming and Shaming of Purity Culture

It was fall football season in the 1980s at Eastwood Baptist High School, and it was a Friday. Students always loved Fridays. Team lockers were decorated for Spirit Week, and jersey numbers and confetti spurred players toward victory on the field. Classes would break at two o'clock for an all-school pep rally, which meant less homework and an early start to the weekend. Perhaps most exciting of all, the girls were allowed to wear blue jeans.

Blue jeans were forbidden to girls at Eastwood, a policy written in the school dress code and strictly enforced by the staff. I remember dozens of occasions in which a female student would either not know the rule, forget the rule, or attempt to subvert the rule and try to sneak from class to class without being noticed. (They were always noticed.) Violators weren't simply given a demerit, a stern warning, or extra homework. They were sent straight home to change into more appropriate clothing, even if it meant missing a lunch hour, lecture, or exam. Parents of students without cars were called, and irritated mothers and fathers were forced to taxi the girls home to their bedroom closets and then back to campus. The parents couldn't really complain because the no-jeans-on-girls policy was one of the better-known—and talked-about—policies on campus. Girls' blue jeans were too form-fitting, too suggestive, too sexy—except on Fridays.

From every vantage, the school policy made no sense. Blue jeans were considered so alluring on girls that they required a schoolwide ban, but Jeans Day was also *gifted* to girls as a *reward* when the school was feeling festive about sports or whatever, meaning that the wearing of jeans was a negative thing unless it was a positive thing. Well, which was it? Were jeans a temptation of the flesh or a celebratory perk? How could blue denim pants be both lustful and virtuous, depending on the day? And why did this strict dress code apply only to females while the hundreds of male students looked like a damn Levi's commercial?

Of course, you are already ahead of me here. We are talking about purity culture.

Many religious schools have long implemented strict rules in an attempt to keep teenagers from succumbing to their hormones. (Good luck with that.) Just for kicks, I Googled "Christian school dress code" and was met with hundreds of academy websites listing rigid requirements: No hats. No hoods. No visible tattoos. Piercings only on girls, only at the bottom of the ears, and nothing flamboyant. No shaved hair designs. No insignias, band names, or political messages. Skirt hemlines may not exceed "a dollar bill width above the kneecap while standing." No sweatpants, athletic shorts, pajamas, yoga pants, or leggings. Shirts must completely conceal shoulders, abdomen, back, and cleavage "when sitting, standing, or bending over." No sheer materials. Nothing with holes. Nothing that exposes undergarments. No flip-flops, clogs, or heels higher than one and a half inches. Boots must not come above the knee or "draw undue attention to oneself."

Most of the pages I browsed favored the word *modesty*.

To avoid temptation, lust, and thousands of rule-breakers stewing in detention, some of the more regimented Christian schools require school uniforms, with each student wearing the same shirts, slacks, and dresses (according to gender). Uniforms simplify things, as home-room teachers don't have to measure hemlines to kneecaps with rulers (yes, they frequently do this), and students can't blaspheme Jesus with ungodly heels, long necklines, and Slipknot concert T-shirts.

Interestingly, much of the modesty message is targeted at girls. This trend can also be seen in the Christian Bible:

- "I also want the women to dress modestly, with decency and propriety, adorning themselves, not with elaborate hairstyles or gold or pearls or expensive clothes."
- "[Women] do not let your adorning be external."
- "Charm is deceitful, and beauty is vain, but a woman who fears the Lord is to be praised."[102]

Starting with Eve in the Garden and throughout the whole of the Bible, scripture constantly appoints women as gatekeepers for sexual purity, sirens with the power to lure their victims with provocative clothing, alluring curves, the bewitching gaze. A woman in Proverbs "dressed as a prostitute." Jezebel "painted her eyes and adorned her head." The daughters of Zion were "haughty and walk with outstretched necks, glancing wantonly with their eyes."[103] The apocalyptic prophecy of Revelation 17 warns about a blasphemous woman carrying a cup of "abominations and the impurities of her sexual immorality." Young girls are taught these scriptures and are preconditioned for guilt, internal conflict, sexual shame, and submission.

Sure, there are many Bible verses that speak to men, but even those commands often revert to females. When Matthew 5:28 says that "anyone who looks at a woman lustfully has already committed adultery with her in his heart," it implies that the female is the object of lust, a magnet that lures a man toward destruction. (Also note that this verse condemns thought crime; Jesus knows when something turns you on.)

For an extreme example of this kind of thinking, we need only to glance toward another Abrahamic religion, fundamentalist Islam, which cloaks its women in burqas and niqabs, full-body coverings that sometimes shield the entire face under a cloth mesh screen. Hardline modesty laws are strictly enforced in Islamist nations such as Iran, Pakistan, and Afghanistan, as commanded in the Qur'an:

> And tell the believing women to restrain their looks, and to *guard their privates*, and *not display their beauty* except what is apparent thereof, and to draw their *coverings over their breasts*, and *not expose their beauty* except to their husbands, their fathers, their husbands' fathers, their sons, their husbands' sons, their brothers, their brothers' sons, their sisters' sons, their women, what their right hands possess, their male attendants who have no sexual desires, or children who are not yet aware of the nakedness of women. And they should not strike their feet to draw attention to their hidden beauty. And repent to God, all of you believers, so that you may succeed. (Qur'an 24:31) (emphasis mine)

In both Islamic and Christian purity culture, notice the conspicuous obsession with sexuality and attraction, and observe how religious purity laws are so often female-focused.

Now, I want to carefully address an aspect of male sexuality that relates to purity culture, making clear that *I am not absolving men of responsibility for their words and actions*. Having said that, it is a biological reality that men, more than women, are usually genetically coded to respond to visual cues for attraction. In the primate world, as a sexually mature male scans for markers of evolutionary fitness, he lights up at the sight of physicality, youth, and beauty because a vibrant, healthy female body is more apt to produce healthy offspring. This is true for lower primates, such as chimpanzees and gorillas. This is true for human primates. (For a deeper dive on this subject, I strongly recommend reading *The Evolution of Desire: Strategies of Human Mating*[104] by evolutionary psychologist David Buss.)

Given our biological makeup, we can see how males autorespond to the sight of attractive females. (With apologies, I am speaking here only to heterosexual attraction, but as approximately 94 percent of the human population is straight,[105] it remains my focus in the context of purity culture. Natural same-sex attractions throughout the animal kingdom are a discussion for another day.)

Now, the fact that these traits and tendencies exist in the human primate does not mean that we haven't evolved the conscious ability to supersede evolved tendencies. In other words, a destructive instinct may still be an instinct, but the human primate can override darker parts of its genetic programming. As Dr. Buss writes:

> The naturalistic fallacy confuses a *scientific description* of human behavior with a *moral prescription* for that behavior. In nature, however, there are diseases, plagues, parasites, infant mortality, and a host of other natural events that we try to eliminate or reduce. The fact that they *do* exist in nature does not imply that they *should* exist.[106]

In this light, the civilized human primate male can experience and acknowledge the evolutionary triggers that draw his eyes toward a beautiful woman *while choosing not to entertain and engage in objectification, obsession, or predation.* In other words, evolved men should be able to think, She's gorgeous! without becoming creepy or predatory.

Sadly, *creepy* and *predatory* remain epidemic adjectives, especially in unenlightened cultures in which men still see women as objects to possess, conquests to boast about, a scapegoat to blame. Human history—and the Christian Bible—have been saturated with dominant men eager to blame (or punish) the liberated woman.

I am reminded of the character of Lilith, known in Judaic tradition as the first wife of the biblical Adam. Created from dust like the man, Lilith was Adam's equal, had a free spirit, was proudly sexual; her independence ultimately resulted in her exit from the garden to produce demonic offspring. Adam needed a sexually virtuous secondary, not a temptress with a mind and body of her own, and this thinking remains in many religious cultures today.

Here is an example. An uncomfortably rapey lip-sync video was shown at the Latter Day Saints' 2013 Sandy Lone Peak State Young Women Standards Night in Utah (ugh . . . that event needs a nickname). Featuring teen guys wearing dress shirts and neckties, the video repurposes the One Direction song "You Don't Know You're Beautiful" with a message to schoolgirls about their bodies. The Mormon version is titled "Virtue Makes You Beautiful." Check out these lyrics:

> Dressing modest, we know it's rough
> When the world's making it so tough.
> Don't need short skirts, or low-cut shirts
> Being the way that you are is enough.

Everyone else doesn't seem to care
Everyone else but you.
Baby you light up the world like nobody else
By the way that you speak and respect yourself.
Girls with integrity are hard to find these days.
You gotta know, oh oh, you are so beautiful.
If only you saw what I can see
You'd understand why I need your modesty.
Right now I'm talking to you, and you must believe
You gotta know, oh oh, virtue is so beautiful.[107]

"You'd understand *why I need your modesty*"??? That is a terrifying statement if you follow it to its implication. The boys are telling the girls, Don't tempt me, honey, because I might not be able to control myself.

Another creepy phenomenon in Christian circles is the Purity Ball. Across the United States, evangelical parents force their children to endure chastity rituals where teens and pre-teens pledge sexual fidelity—not directly to a groom but to their *fathers*. Many of the children are dressed in actual wedding gowns. There is formal entrance and exit music. There are preachers or priests. There is a ring exchange. And there are vows. Here is an actual example of a Purity Ball pledge:

Father speaking: "Dear [Daughter], This is the day of the Purity Ball. We are so excited. This ring is made of gold, a precious metal, and shaped into a heart, and it signifies how precious your heart is to God, to us, and to your future husband, who God is preparing for you. The diamond chip is a sign of purity, a reminder that you are committing to purity in heart, soul, mind, and body until marriage. You will be able to give your husband the gift of purity, rare and precious."

The father slips a band onto the child's left ring finger, and the daughter puts a band on her dad's right ring finger. The rings represent the child's promise to remain a virgin until marriage. Roses are placed. Fathers of all daughters form a circle on a dance floor. Hands are placed on the children.

All fathers speaking [after a brief preamble]: "We pray a wall of protection around our girls that they would not give in to a moment that will destroy their lives. Father, guard the feminine, vulnerable, dependent spirits that You created in them. May fathers stand tall and war for the souls of their daughters and remain faithful to protect these girls for generations to come."[108]

See the loaded language? The ceremony focuses on female obedience. The girls are "dependent." Female purity is a gift to the husband, and sexual promiscuity (adultery!) will likely "destroy their lives." Given that girls usually begin puberty around the age of eleven, and given that the average age for marriage in the United States is thirty-one,[109] we are looking at two full decades during which sexually mature people will grapple with innate, natural desires prohibited to them. Don't spoil the merchandise! Don't break your promise! Keep yourself pure! (Again, notice that in this strict biblical model for sexual fidelity, the females are accountable to males.)

A similar Christian chastity campaign is the popular "True Love Waits" model. TLW started in the 1990s as a series of virginity pledges, also involving rings, in which teenagers and college students—most often girls—promise abstinence until marriage. The pledge reads: "Believing that true love waits, I make a commitment to God, myself, my family, my friends, my future mate, and my future children to be sexually abstinent from this day until the day I enter a biblical marriage relationship."[110]

(A quick aside. Note that when the time for marriage does come, Christian tradition includes the ceremonial line, "Who gives this woman to be wed?" which again exposes Christianity's model of the subservient female. It is a man who *gives away* the bride.)

TLW is alarming on a number of levels. Its oath is linked to "biblical marriage," which is actually terrifying. Have you *seen* the marriages in the Bible? Yahweh is just fine with all of the following scenarios:

- One man + one woman (Adam and Eve, etc.)[111]

- One man + wife + the man's concubines (The biblical concubine was essentially an unmarried sex doll. Abraham, Gideon, Jacob, Solomon, and other "godly" men enjoyed boinking their mistresses.)[112]

- One man + wife + the wife's slaves (Abraham fathered a kid with Sarah's female slave. C'mon! The old wife wouldn't conceive!)[113]

- One man + wife + wife + wife, etc. (Esau, David, Solomon, Belshazzar, and others were polygamists.)[114]

- One man + his rape victim (In his wisdom and fairness, God required the rapist to pay fifty shekels of silver to the raped woman's dad.)[115]

- One man + his kidnapped virgin (Yahweh allowed his Israelite soldiers to spare female virgins from execution so they could be kidnapped as wives.)[116]

How does the God-is-love crowd rationalize their biblical heroes shagging everything but the sheep? Not well. But apologists have a "Get Out of Consistency Free" card, explaining that biblical times normalized having, say, seven hundred wives, and that Yahweh was simply using the sexual exploits of Old Testament heroes to accomplish a greater good. Of course, it is no accident that these pathetic excuses were written by men, and Christianity still leans heavily on biblical double standards and chastity teachings showered upon the young. Keep the faith. Say the pledge. Confess the sin. Distrust your nature. Desire is the Devil's calling card.

Set up for failure, purity-culture kids are plunged through puberty and into sexual maturity already feeling ashamed and guilty for normal thoughts and inclinations. Teenagers often betray their purity oaths in the heat of the moment, become wracked with guilt and feelings of failure, and then either bury their shame in misery or submit themselves to a religious authority to pay for their carnal crimes. Many are shamed by family and friends, guilted into penitence rituals, or dragged before whole congregations to apologize. Some girls and boys jump prematurely into the marriage bed rather than become adulteresses and adulterers, as commanded in the Bible: "But if they cannot control themselves, they should marry, for it is better to marry than to burn with passion."[117] As such, many young people have weddings before they have careers, stable homes, or even a bearing on their own identities, values, goals, and dreams.

A bizarre practice in some Christian churches revolves around "accountability partners." Perhaps following the sponsor model in Alcoholics Anonymous, teens experiencing sexual thoughts and temptations are encouraged to (I am not kidding) call or visit their accountability partner to confess and ask for prayers, as sexual desire has activated their loins. The prayer is supposed to produce a cold-shower effect as God cools the blood, and the now-sexually disinterested party can return to not thinking about lusting and thrusting. A Tulsa church took this tragic scenario to the next level with (I am still not kidding) "masturbation partners," which isn't what you might think. Young people in the church tempted to self-pleasure are charged *to let another person talk them out of it*. What would that conversation even *sound* like?

I am not saying that devout Christians can't be sincere, good people who try to shield their children from perceived harm, especially given the implications of pregnancy and STDs (which is a sex education issue, not a sin issue). I am saying that the practice of purity culture is an oxymoron. It seeks to desexualize people even as it remains *totally obsessed* with sexuality. You simply cannot be free of something you obsess over. As Fyodor Dostoevsky wrote in 1863, "Try to pose for yourself this task: not to think of a polar bear, and you will see that the cursed thing will come to mind every minute."

In other words, the sex sermonizers are kidding themselves. They might as well be telling people not to breathe, eat, or sleep.

Interestingly, Christian sex "education" has been so ineffective that the Bible Belt states of Arkansas, Mississippi, Louisiana, Oklahoma, and Alabama lead the nation in teen pregnancies.[118] PornHub released its 2017 report congratulating the United States for being its biggest global customer. A 2009 Harvard analysis of credit card data ranked the largely Mormon state of Utah as the top national consumer for pornography,[119] and porn use is on the rise in southern evangelical hubs.[120] For those wondering about the efficacy of school dress codes, "schoolgirl uniform" remains a commonly searched fetish category in the adult porn industry.

So, what about those girl students at Eastwood Baptist School? They simply shifted from form-fitting blue jeans to form-fitting denim of another color or tight slacks in a different fabric, defiantly outsmarting the rule makers. Skirts measured the required no-more-than three inches above the knee, but the dresses still hugged the curvy female form. Girls buttoned up their blouses to the required height, but there was no hiding their innate femininity and beauty. In fact, moral prohibitions accidentally created a forbidden-fruit scenario in which attempts at repression backfired. The more those attractions were discouraged, the stronger they became.

I couldn't help but wonder if Eastwood's moral overlords themselves wrestled with thoughts deemed impure. Were their rules secretly redirected at their own conflicted hearts? How many of them had hidden kinks, a history of backseat trysts, or sexual dysfunction branded onto them by their own parents and cultures?

As a Christian teenager, I hadn't taken a formal purity pledge in the sense of ceremonies and rings, but I had still promised God to abstain from sexual sins. I then propelled out of puberty into a feedback loop of frustrations and failure. My young, supercharged, sexual self ached with desire—often resulting in awkwardness, sometimes in embarrassment, and almost always with guilt and shame. I didn't understand my own body, let alone the female body. I was never properly educated about attraction mechanisms, reproductive systems, organs, or orgasms. Any references to sex education used vague vocabulary pinned to Bible verses. We students didn't learn about our bodies; we learned to be ashamed of them.

I remained a virgin until eighteen, but the preceding years saw me (and my girlfriends) pushing sexual desires to the very edge of intercourse, and when the heat of the moment waned, I would beg God to forgive me for being so weak and carnal. "Forgive me, Lord, for my sin. I promise that I will never do it again." Days later, I would do it again. This is the tragic shame cycle that results from purity culture, with stories like this rampant among former evangelicals. Christianity had called them sexually sick, and of course, the church was selling the cure. Sin and repent. Sin and repent. Sin and repent. Some people never escape this hamster wheel.

Yet there has never been a verse, doctrine, pledge, ring, or article of clothing that has canceled out the sexual side of the human condition. Blame it. Shame it. Repress it. Cover it. Prohibit it. Sex isn't going away, and the religious chastity crowd is harming good people who deserve better than to be desexualized by ignorant Iron Age patriarchs and the defenders of their words.

I am no Alfred Kinsey, but my fifty-plus years on this Earth (including the time since my exit from religion in 2008) have produced some perspective, and if I had a time machine, my advice to my freshly activated teenage self would be this:

- **Ignore the Bible.** If you will pardon the expression, Christianity knows fuck-all about sex. The Bible's authors were constantly on the wrong side of cosmology, geology, meterology, history, and almost everything else addressed in its "truths." Why would anyone think the bibical take on sex is reliable? Its Old Testament begins with the tragic claim that Eve's sexual desire (and thus the sexual desire of all female descendants) was a curse for tempting Adam. In its New Testament, God's salvation plan required nonconsensual ghost sex with an unwed teenager. Front to back, from incest to virgin rapes to angel coupling and beyond, the Bible's bed-hopping characters were poster children for ignorance and sexual dysfunction, their stories the mere written words of anonymous, primitive, and patriarchal men. Taking sex advice from Bible authors is like learning modern astrophysics from the scribblings of first-century astrologers.

- **Own it.** Sexual desires and attractions are perfectly natural and normal. Study the human primate so that you can understand how sexual drive is activated at puberty and impacts you throughout your life. At the very least, recognize that your biology isn't broken. Sexuality exists for a reason, and that reason isn't sin. Whatever you do, don't get sex ed from a church; seek out actual experts on science and human sexuality.

- **Do solo runs.** Regarding the puritans who shout "thou shalt not masturbate," I would wager than many of those primates are quite likely spanking their own monkey. Self-pleasure is simply pleasure. It is not shredding the moral fabric of humanity. It won't spoil you for relationships. It is not the betrayal of a future spouse (or a current one). The majority of males do it, as do the majority of females. (Statista's polls reveal that more than 80 percent of young and middle-aged men self-pleasure, as do about 67 percent of like-aged women.[121])

  Despite the urban legends, you won't grow hair on your hands. You won't go blind. God isn't making an incriminating sex tape of you for Judgment Day. Masturbation feels good, it relaxes you, it can improve sleep, it greatly reduces the likelihood of STDs, it can build confidence as you discover your own body, and perhaps best of all, you can inform conservative evangelicals that your purchase of lubes and sex toys boosts capitalism.

- **Have premarital sex.** (Man, I can hear the religious berserkers losing their shit over this one.) A background of sexual experience doesn't make you an adulterer, nor is it the church's business. Learn to protect yourself emotionally and physically, and as a responsible and liberated person, enjoy what you enjoy. If your eventual spouse isn't your first sexual partner, fine. If you are sexing it up with your fiancé before the nuptials, fine. Beyond that, if you decide that marriage just isn't your thing, congratulations on defining who you are and what you want, on your own terms.

- **Live with someone before marrying them.** How many people have grappled with and suppressed years of innate desires only to discover—too late—that they were trapped in a marriage contract with a sexually incompatible partner? Sexual compatibility is critical; it needs to be determined before committing to marriage, and you and your partner deserve better than to fumble through your honeymoon in the darkness of ignorance. Living together allows you to see each other at your best and worst, it exposes any intimacy issues, and if you do decide to have the wedding, you can make that decision without feeling like you are rushing to be together.

  Beyond that, I have discovered that you don't have to be married to have, and be, a family. Families come in many forms. You don't need a signed piece of paper to have family. Christians can't invalidate your house because it doesn't look like their own, and again, their marriage model was drawn from the kidnap-the-virgin-girls-for-yourselves book. Not exactly a credible source. Just move on and do your thing.

- **Have fun with it.** By nature, I have never been very adventurous, but I have come to realize how much time and energy I once wasted judging those who are. *Kinky* used to be a pejorative in my mind. Today, revulsion of kink no longer binds me (if you will pardon the expression). Prefer the missionary position? Fine. Want to hang from the ceiling in a cat suit? Whatever works. Prefer multiple partners, same-sex partners, a smorgasbord of varied partners? Knock yourself out. If all parties are within the law, do no harm, and give enthusiastic consent, sex is a sandbox in which imagination and play should be encouraged.

Beyond the above advice, I think understanding the destructive power of sexual shame is imperative. High-control religions (and cults) want us to feel accountable to them instead of thinking for ourselves, and they often claim the moral authority of God, guilting us for normal thoughts and natural behaviors. They want to regulate what we think, what we wear, who we desire, and how we express that desire. They don't have the right to do this, and we don't owe them permission, no matter how often they assure us that they are acting "in the love of Christ" for our physical and spiritual well-being.

Love needs no religion, and sexual expression needs no clerical stamp of approval. In this light, beginning in youth and throughout our lives, we can embrace the sexual self as not just healthy and wonderful but also as the defiant rebuke of meddling moralists demanding the keys to our private spaces.

CHAPTER ELEVEN
Come Lord Jesus – Anxieties of the Earthbound Believer

Ask an American Christian to describe Heaven, and the responses you get will be as unique as the individuals you ask. Some talk about mansions and pearly gates. Some focus almost exclusively on Jesus. Some speak in more abstract terms about energy, light, music, and joy. But the idea of Heaven is universally presented as an absolute leveling-up from this troubled, conflicted, mortal world.

I am reminded of a live concert recording by the late Christian songwriter Keith Green. He said that Earth would be a garbage can compared to Heaven. The crowd cheered.

Think about how people use the adjective *heavenly* to describe delightful things, from sunsets to songs to chocolate cake. Heaven is perceived as an absolute good, a place of mind-blowing bliss just beyond the earthly horizon. Ask a believer if they are looking forward to Heaven, and there is little doubt you will hear anything but an enthusiastic *Yes!*

Yet my (admittedly unscientific) observations of the church reveal a culture often steeped in fear about death, the gateway to Heaven. Here in red-state Oklahoma, many of the same people who get misty-eyed about their eternal reward are obsessed with preventing death. From deadbolts to stun guns to shotguns, their lives are lived in a persistent fear of physical harm and lethal threats, despite biblical instructions to never be afraid. The scriptures are clear:

- "And do not fear those who kill the body but cannot kill the soul."
- ". . . for God gave us a spirit not of fear, but of power and love and self-control."
- "So we can confidently say, "The Lord is my helper; I will not fear; what can man do to me?"[122]

Believers give lip service to these notions of divine protection, but notice how they shield themselves from perceived (and real) dangers as if no God exists. From parking lot muggers, home burglars, and government coups to the Antichrist, jeopardy seems to loom over the American Christian, so the safe housing and stockpiling begin. Sure, the God that cares for even the sparrows of the sky[123] watches over his children, but it can't hurt to install those motion sensor alarms at every exposed door. Lethal harm is everywhere, and there is a palpable fear of death, no matter how appealing the Sunday preachers try to make Heaven sound.

When I was a Christian, Heaven existed only in the abstract. Depictions of Heaven were always homogenous oil paintings with gold light, winged angels, a gilded gate, puffy clouds, and, of course, Jesus looking like the cover of a Yanni album. That Heaven always seemed impersonal to me. I couldn't connect with it. In fact, despite its many problems, Earth was always more appealing, with more color and culture contrasts, more tangible contact with people and things, and a sharper focus on living instead of singing and shouting, "Holy holy holy is the Lord God Almighty." Heaven didn't feel real. Even biblical descriptions of beautiful mansions and pearly gates sounded like a gaudy soundstage for the Trinity Broadcasting Network, somehow both ostentatious and bland, and certainly not very appealing.

For me, Heaven was attractive only because I wanted to live beyond death and because I liked the idea of seeing my long-lost loved ones again. But there was no urgency to get there, and I certainly didn't want to check out early. No, it was important—critical—to keep myself alive here on planet Earth for as long as possible, and so it is with most Christians who have booby-trapped their lives to prevent premature entrance into Glory.

Beyond the jitters about daily dangers lie the constant warnings about the End Times. History is loaded with draconian rants about fulfilled prophecies and crimson moons, wars and rumors of wars, and the global machinations that will trigger the apocalypse. The Oxford English Dictionary defines *apocalypse* as "the complete final destruction of the world as described in the biblical book of Revelation," but most believers remain convinced that they will be long gone before that meat grinder begins. Yes, the planet will experience chaos in advance of Christ's return, but the worst of the wars, plagues, curses, blood, and suffering will occur after God's children are raptured into Heaven.

If you believe in Heaven, this sounds like a pretty good transaction: a little bit of tumult in exchange for perfect bliss—but you wouldn't know it by talking to believers constantly torqued in fear. From the death of a pope to the election of a president, with almost every military conflict, every major natural disaster, every terrorist attack, and every horrific headline, the faithful do the following:

1) See a sign of the End Times.
2) Freak out.

In this regard, Christians make no sense. If their anticipation of Heaven is genuine, they should greet every sign with praises and parties. They are one step closer to Paradise. Jesus's return is imminent. Perfect joy is just around the bend. Yet there is often only trepidation and handwringing as the pulpit pounders warn their flocks about the danger and doom. The church then maneuvers to try to reverse, or at least mitigate, the effects of these End Times precursors, acting to delay Revelation's inevitabilities and prolong the church's days here on Earth.

Some might argue that they are simply grieved about the billions of unsaved people and so they are nudging back the apocalypse to buy time for evangelism, but let's face reality: most Christians are not personally excited about the destruction of their earthly life in advance of a heavenly life. They give lip service to Heaven (especially at funerals, where promises of reunion bring comfort), but they clutch onto the physical world in white-knuckled desperation.

Apocalyptic narratives frequently infect American Christian gun culture, where evangelicals huff about divine protection at the trigger end of their pistols and AR-15 rifles. Theirs is a paranoid fear fantasy of impending Christian jihad. In their "God Votes Republican" T-shirts, these conspiratorial fraidy cats can't even visit a Starbucks without firearms in their belts and handbags. Jeopardy looms always, and God's Minute Men must be vigilant and ready for battle—even over morning coffee. Journalist, author, and screenwriter Jon Niccum, referring to a recent published study, writes, "Whether it's a fear of violence or a steadfast belief in constitutional rights, Americans have strong opinions on why they need guns. But concerns about Satan and Armageddon also enter their decision-making."[124] Those primed to see encroaching danger will latch on to almost anything scary, their long laundry list of trigger words including foreigner, immigrant, liberal, communist, socialist, secularist, humanist, and, of course, atheist.

If physical death is indeed the quick ticket to Paradise, why are these heavily armed evangelicals not dropping their weapons, painting targets on their chests, running toward their perceived enemies, and crying, "Take me?" Even if their physical bodies were struck down by Satan himself, wouldn't they immediately gain residency in the vastly better cosmic wonderland of peace, joy, color, love, and light?

I think it is interesting how Christian culture is so often a culture of locked doors and loaded guns. Believers ostensibly safeguarded by Yahweh nervously turn their deadbolts, click their seatbelts, reinforce their safe rooms, install their shelters, build their arsenals, and do everything in their power to prevent the Heaven they breathlessly promote. In effect, they are fortifying a rotted outhouse to avoid their inheritance of Buckingham Palace. This behavior only makes sense if we realize and acknowledge that when the chips are down, Christians may not actually believe the things they profess. Despite all of the lip service about divine protection, they are not relying on God to save them, and they certainly don't behave like people eager to begin the next life. They entrench their position on planet Earth, shouting the conflicting claims: We're protected. We're in danger! We're secure. We're under attack! It's the End Times (smiles). It's the End Times (screams)! And all the while, they scramble to avoid the perfect Heaven, which is ostensibly the happy ending—or beginning—of their lives. Death is the gateway, and believers are running in the opposite direction.

I am reminded of the 2009 documentary *Religulous*, in which Bill Maher speaks with a devout Christian:

Maher: "You're 100 percent sure that, after you die, you'll go to a better place?"

Man: "I know I'll be with God. I'll be with Jesus."

Maher: "And that's a better place."

Man: "Um. Even if it was in a garbage can, I know it won't be, but even if it was, just the fact that I'm with Jesus—to me—is good."

Maher: "It's a better place."

Man: "It's a better place."

Maher: "Then why don't you kill yourself?"

Maher didn't get a response. I know that Christianity—especially Catholicism—considers suicide a sin, but Maher's point remains a good one. Mainstream believers aren't ramping up the odds and opportunities for an early check-out. They speak Heaven but they live Earth, and this desperation to hold on to their mortal coils exposes where their feet are planted: right here, in the real world.

To this rule, there are certainly many exceptions. Beyond extremist death cults such as Heaven's Gate and Jonestown, the latter of which literally force-fed their followers a rendezvous in Heaven, we do see examples of misty-eyed Christians focused only on the afterlife. As the Bible declares that "no one knows the day or hour when these things will happen,"[125] any and every day could be The Day—the anticipated Second Coming of Christ. This anticipation of Heaven then governs how believers act and react on Earth as they scramble to prepare and gaze at the horizon. Yet even these people aren't immune to fear and frenzy, their joy about perfect Eternity tempered by the horrors of Revelation.

If nothing else, many waste their earthly existence in constant preparation for Life 2.0, unable to prove Heaven but committing long decades in the service of it. I find this terribly tragic; people are essentially living for dying.

I don't have much else to say in this short chapter. Mostly, I want to encourage you to observe the words-versus-actions behaviors of Christians perpetually paranoid about the End of Days. They cry Come Lord Jesus as they work feverishly to push back the mechanisms for Christ's return. They preach confidence as they act with insecurity and trepidation about every headline. They claim victory yet incessantly warn of the encroaching enemy. God may be everywhere, but the Devil could be anywhere, and this contradicting attitude becomes a self-cancelling noise. The afterlife might be a perfect place of painless bliss, but tellingly, many Christians constantly maneuver to avoid it. For them, Earth is home, and Heaven can wait.

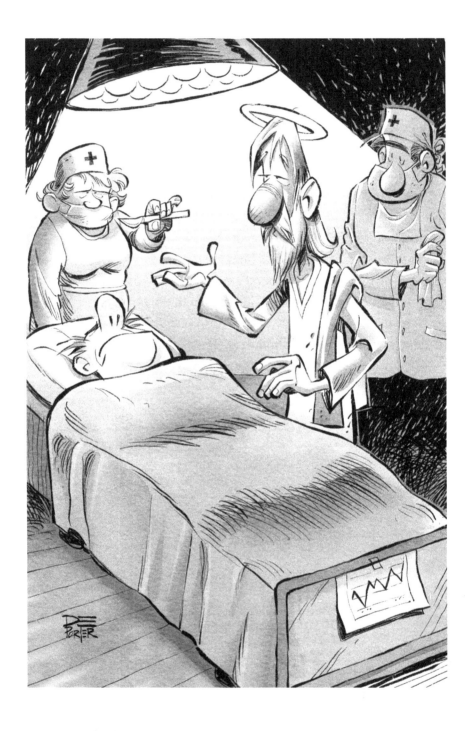

CHAPTER TWELVE
The Hands of the Surgeon – Healing, Hypocrisy, and the Church

I have done a lot of lighthearted poking at my former religion in this book, but if you will indulge me, I need to be a bit more serious here because these issues can be serious, and while I am not going to shy away from the (il)logic at work, I also don't want to surrender my compassion for those experiencing dark days—specifically those calling down the power of prayer.

At the June 2017 Imagine No Religion 7 conference in Toronto, I spoke about the strange relationship between Christian prayer warriors and their many, many doctors. The scenario I used then, which I will use again here, begins with a diagnosis: an operable tumor. A carcinoma. Cancer.

In the wake of this terrible news, a treatment plan is set: surgery and chemotherapy. Families and friends desperately pray for healing, even as they scramble to find the most qualified physician available. They pray as the operation is scheduled. They pray as the patient is prepped. They pray as the gurney is wheeled into surgery. And as the doctor wields his scalpel, they ask Jesus to "please guide the hands of the surgeon."

This is a difficult issue to broach because challenging these behaviors can seem callous and cold in the shadow of desperation and suffering. In desperate moments, given our very human need for hope and comfort, calling down divine favor is understandable behavior. Many times (and I know this is difficult for many atheists to accept), the act of praying can have a calming, even meditative effect on those who are traumatized. Even if no One is on the receiving end of the call, ritual prayers can balm the senses. Dr. David Spiegel, Associate Chair of Psychiatry and Behavioral Sciences at Stanford, explains it this way:

> Praying involves the deeper parts of the brain: the medial prefrontal cortex and the posterior cingulate cortex—the midfront and back portions. . . . These parts of the brain are involved in self-reflection and self-soothing.[126]

In other words, prayer can have a medicating effect, especially in times of trouble. It fires up the prefrontal cortex, the thalamus, and parietal lobe as neurotransmitters reduce anxiety.[127] When humans speak toward the heavens, they often enjoy a dose of their own medicine. Psychologist Tanya Luhrmann agrees:

> People stay with this God not because the theology makes sense, but because the practice delivers emotionally. When you feel lousy, reaching out to this God helps you to feel better.[128]

Dr. Luhrmann makes the case that prayer doesn't have to be reasonable to be emotionally beneficial, but I consider this approach to prayer a bit naïve because, in many instances, prayer can result in feelings of confusion, inadequacy, and shame. As ex-pastor Dan Barker famously said, "Nothing fails like prayer."

More on that later. I want to return to my hypothetical example about the loved one stricken with cancer, their family begging God to guide the surgeon's knife. My example begins with a fictional doctor named Patricia Blackwell.

Decades ago, Patricia went to college to complete a four-year pre-med undergraduate degree, which involved intense study in the fields of chemistry, anatomy, biology, and physics. She studied her ass off to pass the Medical College Admission Test (MCAT) before being accepted to medical school, which was another four-year grind involving intense studies of anatomy, biochemistry, pharmacology, physiology, and more. She was then required to pass the medical equivalent of the Bar Exam, called the United States Medical Licensing Examination, before beginning a grueling five-year residency, complete with twenty-hour shifts and a sixty-month sacrifice of almost every non-medical person and interest in her life. Yet Dr. Blackwell still wasn't finished because she had another two-year fellowship in her specialized field of surgical oncology. Her education represents thousands of hours of study, training, and testing, and accrued student loan amounts higher than the asking price of some luxury homes.

Dr. Patricia Blackwell has been a practicing surgical oncologist for twenty-six years. She is also an atheist.

Our second hypothetical character is Dr. Stephanie Frazier:

Dr. Frazier is a devout Christian. She believes strongly in the healing power of prayer. She names and claims God's promise: "This is the confidence we have in approaching God: that if we ask anything according to his will, he hears us. And if we know that he hears us—whatever we ask—we know that we have what we asked of him."[129]

Dr. Stephanie Frazier is not a surgical oncologist. She is a dentist.

Now, if the naming-and-claiming prayer warriors were forced to choose between these two doctors, which physician would they most trust to care for their beloved son, daughter, father, mother, cousin, friend, co-worker, neighbor, or even a passerby on the street? I suspect they would soon find themselves in Dr. Blackwell's examination room after telling Stephanie Frazier DDS, "Uh, do I have teeth in my cancerous colon? If not, please go away."

But why choose the atheist? If their trust is in God and the Lord indeed guides the hands of the proxy-surgeons, wouldn't it make more sense for a spiritually attuned fellow Christian to do the work at hand?

And what does the guide-the-hand-of-the-surgeon scenario even look like? How is a surgery *without* the prayers any different from the surgery *with* the prayers? Do the doctors notice a difference? Does one surgeon suddenly jump away from the table and yell, "Oh, shit! We forgot to say the magic words!"? For those of us who grew up playing the popular kids' game Operation, I am reminded of this popular internet meme:

Yet even as we smirk (or recoil) at this little piece of blasphemy, the meme speaks to some legitimate questions about God's master plan and challenges to the power of prayer. Why all these third-party "miracles?"

Throughout scripture, God healed his children directly. Yahweh restored Naaman the leper. Christ miraculously stopped a woman's "discharge of blood" and cured the hobbled legs of the crippled man. Jesus used magic mud to restore sight to the blind man and even reanimated the dead body of Lazarus. The New Testament tells us that "Jesus went to every town and village. He taught in their meeting places and preached the good news about God's kingdom. Jesus also healed every kind of disease and sickness."[130]

The Bible's promises of healing remain for God's children today. "Whatever you ask in prayer, you will receive, if you have faith." "Whatever you ask in my name, this I will do, that the Father may be glorified in the Son. If you ask me anything in my name, I will do it."[131] This seems straightforward. Jesus mentions no surgeons. No secondhand agents. No proxies. Sure, there are Bible stories about secondhand miracles, but when the moment is dire, especially considering the time, angst, pain, and often bankrupting expense of invasive surgery, why wouldn't Jesus simply eliminate the middleman and pass the healing right on to the consumer?

Our culture is loaded with self-professed faith healers declaring themselves extensions of God's healing hands. Interestingly, they conduct their services in convention centers instead of hospitals, and their "miracles" never involve those with totally debilitating afflictions, missing limbs, and so on.

I once saw a billboard for Florida Hospital Waterman that ironically declared FAITH > CANCER. This same hospital charges huge fees for the physical treatment of cancer. So is faith the mechanism for healing, or is it a trained scientist bringing decades of training and experience in his specialized field? Is faith supposed to give the doctors some kind of nifty power-up, like in a video game? From the outside, how could we discern which maladies are cured by doctors and which are cured by God?

When I was a Christian radio broadcaster, we ran advertisements for a chiropractor with the word-salad tagline: "Doctors treat; God heals." *This makes no sense!* If God does the healing, why are doctors prescribing treatment? Along those same lines, I was recently sent the link to a Facebook page called "Stop Cancer. Start Praying," where a commenter shared the inspiring story of a supernatural healing:[132]

> I must tell all of you, God does heal cancer! My wife had stage 4c Ovarian Psammocarcinoma. With prayer and faith, and chemo treatments for a yr1/2 she is 100% cancer free. The emphasise is faith. You really have to have a faith support system to help you stay strong. Many people will pray without faith, thus you have negative results. Many people who have posted such unbelief in God sound as though they have atheistic values, which is sad to see. Your point on God sounds as though you yourself have had a loss in your own life, thus blaming God for losing someone in the same manner. The Bible, the word of God says that healing is the children's bread. God desires to heal everyone. Satan, the Devil, comes to steal(souls), kill(lives), and destroy(God's creation). Cancer is not of God! However if people blatantly want to deny God, why should he heal them?God is a God of love. Yes he knew about

Prayer. Faith. And eighteen months of chemo. Is this our standard for answered healing prayers? What happened to the touched cloak, the healing rivers, the magic mud, each of which produced an immediate result without Jesus turning to the disciples and saying, "Go fetch the nurse, some rubbing alcohol, and a sharp rock"? Are contemporary Christians saying that God's personal touch ended with his New Testament ascension? Are they bending themselves into pretzel shapes to accommodate this notion of secondhand miracles, ones that require insurance policies with obscene deductibles, arduous tests, invasive scalpels, scientifically developed medicines, punishing recovery regimens, and often lackluster results? (Notice how often a believer praises God for a cancer in remission but not irrevocably cured.)

Since I have already opened Pandora's Box on the subject, I must also ask the broader question about the very purpose of prayers because the act of praying implies that an all-knowing, all-wise God needs to be convinced to change his mind. Why would an omniscient deity ever require convincing? In this light, calls to prayer begin to take on a darker and more sinister shade because they reveal the troubling picture of a god that holds hostage the cures for disease until the proper petitions are laid at his feet. He can fix the problem with a blink, but first he wants us to beg.

Apologists like to argue that God already knows that the prayers are incoming, so he has allowed for answered prayers in advance. In that light, God doesn't actually change his mind; his mind already knew how the scenario would play out.

Still others laser-focus only on the actual act of praying. For them, the results aren't as important as obediently groveling at the feet of the Almighty. If answers to prayers arrive, they are considered a bonus. After all, sinful humans don't really deserve the goodness of God, which makes his random beneficence more wonderful.

I don't know how else to emphasize this except to literally underline it: <u>Omniscient God knows all cures for cancer.</u> These cures are at the fore of his mind, on the tip of his tongue, in the palm of his all-powerful hand. Yet in the wake of desperate human pleading (and 9.2 million cancer deaths every year[133]), God chooses not to appear in all his glory, chooses not to wave his arms across every home and hospital to instantly eradicate all cancer cells. Instead, he hides himself inside tiny chemotherapy needles, his presence so slight that observers cannot distinguish which tumors are killed by chemo and which are killed by Christ. As the desperate patient has a port punched into his chest, his body withers, his hair falls out, neuropathy destroys nerves in his hands and feet, and he vomits more food than he digests. Healthy cells die alongside the cancer cells as the victim becomes a mere shell of himself, and all the while, he and his loved ones continue their desperate cries toward the sky, blaming the cancer for the bad days and praising Jesus for the good ones.

Actually, the victims and families don't always blame the cancer. Sometimes they blame the doctors. Or the Devil. Or, in the most tragic cases, they even blame themselves. I will return to this point in a moment.

Fundamental Christianity has several built-in protective mechanisms against scrutiny and criticism, and this is certainly true when it comes to prayer. I sometimes use another hypothetical situation to illustrate how this works. Imagine an innocent teenager wounded in a drive-by gang shooting.

- If the bullets completely miss the teenager, Christians declare it a miracle. God guided the projectiles away from his body.
- If the boy is mildly wounded, God is thanked because the result could have been so much worse. A flesh wound is better than a vital organ wound. God protected the heart, lungs, and brain. It is still a miracle.
- If the boy is struck in the spine and paralyzed, God is thanked

for sparing his life. He could have been killed outright, so it is a wonder that he survived at all. Satan's murderers were thwarted. Against all odds, the boy remains alive, and perhaps God is even using this earthly "light and momentary affliction"[134] to produce an eternal result that will bring greater glory to the Father.

- If the teen dies of his wounds, the family (likely) doesn't blame God, but instead speaks the biblical promise that "we know all things work together for good to them that love God, to them who are called according to his purpose."[135] Everything happens for a reason, and sometimes those reasons make no sense to pithy humans. We can't understand. We are not even supposed to understand. Sure, it seems horrible and wasteful and brutal and tragic, but take comfort in knowing that God has a plan, and best of all, the family will one day be happily reunited in Heaven.

See how these mechanisms work? There is literally *no* scenario in which God doesn't have an escape hatch. God hears and answers prayer but not necessarily at the moment we pray, nor in the way we expect, nor in a way that can be verified as his work, nor even in our lifetime. The goalposts slide into any and every position, with every possible outcome considered a score—unless people have failed in their faith.

I want to return to this tragic shadow of self-blame because it is so misguided, so unnecessary, and so harmful. The downside of naming and claiming a divine miracle for the sick is the guilt and shame that often follow unanswered prayers. We should have prayed harder. We didn't have enough faith. If only we had been better Christians. Evangelicals have long blamed the Devil's wiles and the tainted human heart for every tragedy in the world, from earthquakes to child leukemia to fatal car accidents, declaring that the original sin of the biblical Adam and Eve cursed all of humankind. Humans are all born wretches. If we are to be worthy and good, we must receive the worthy, good God. This is another powerful shield, as Christianity can take credit for good fortune, positive outcomes, lucky breaks, love and music and rainbows and the healthy smiles of newborn babies— while anything not beautiful is our fault or Satan's evil. Convenient.

Inward blame results in a constant self-flagellation for being born human, for being imperfect, for our natural questions and fears and vulnerabilities. Whether we are afflicted with disease or forced to grieve the affliction of another, our suffering is a result of our sin, and we are all infected with sin.[136]

Finally, we must ask the most obvious question. We have established that the act of praying can produce a meditative sense of calm and even euphoria, but in terms of reversing disease and miraculously healing diseased bodies, does prayer actually work?

In 2006, Dr. Herbert Benson and his team at Harvard University received a $2.4 million grant to study the effects of prayer in cardiac bypass patients.[137] The experiment involved patients at six US hospitals randomly assigned to one of three groups:

Group One: 604 patients were to receive intercessory prayer and were told they *may or may not* receive prayer.

Group Two: 597 patients were to receive *no* intercessory prayer and were told they *may or may not* receive prayer.

Group Three: 601 patients were to receive intercessory prayer and were told they *would* receive prayer.

The prayers for groups one and three started the night before the by-pass procedures, which took place over the course of two weeks. The results were gauged in terms of post-op complications.

Interestingly, those in group one, who received intercession without a prayer guarantee, experienced a 52 percent complication rate. Those who received no intercession and no prayer guarantee experienced a 51 percent complication rate. Not only were the numbers nearly identical, but those who were *not* prayed for actually fared better in their recoveries by a percentage point.

Even more interesting is the finding from group three. Those 601 patients received prayers and knew people were praying for them, yet their post-op complication rate was *59 percent*. These patients fared almost 10 percent worse than the other two groups even though they were aware that they were being lifted up by religious intercessors.

Writing for *Psychology Today*, Dr. Stanton Peele notes a statistical analysis of prayers conducted by Francis Galton. Galton ran patients through a similar prayer gauntlet only to discover that the recovery rates of prayed-for people didn't increase *at all*.[138] In light of the Harvard study, not only do prayers fail to produce positive results, they sometimes make things worse.

Why? Did the unfortunate members of group three feel more pressure to recover knowing they were being prayed for? Did they feel objectified? Did they feel a personal responsibility to improve lest they let everyone down? There is little doubt that prayer recipients can experience tremendous pressure, and any lack of improvement might make them feel like they failed in their faith under the prayers of the faithful. "I didn't get better. It must be my own fault."

Even those who don't blame themselves might be quick to blame, or even sue, the doctors for incompetence or malpractice. Hence, physicians get placed in the lose-lose position of being blamed for bad outcomes, while God is thanked for good ones. Even as they bring decades of education, training, and skill to humanity's medical interventions, doctors are often tragically ignored when the wounds heal, when the tumor shrinks, when the virus dies, when the pieces get put back together. In the dense fog of pleas and praises, the true healers vanish as the faithful shout, "Glory to God, who guided the hands of the surgeon."

My religious days were peppered with these kinds of platitudes. For every fortuitous outcome, I gave God a standing ovation, and when calamity struck, I reflexively looked the other way. I am guilty of having once asked Jesus to supernaturally assist the surgeons—the Healer helping healers. As a Christian radio host, I gave testimonials for Christian doctors claiming that their services were guided by God. I saw no irony as I prayed for intervention with my family physician, a hardcore believer, mere seconds after he prescribed antibiotics for my sore throat, respiratory infection, or chest cold. Time and again I prayed for healing but paid for doctors. Truthfully, I sounded like an idiot, speaking lofty-yet-trite words and phrases that somehow masked the ridiculousness of it all.

And as I am about to reveal, I often spoke in the vacant and often inscrutable language of the American cultural Christian, talking to and about my god in the special language of my fellow believers.

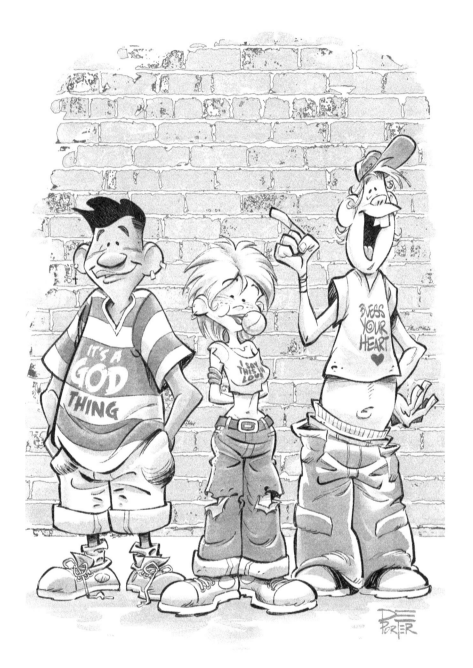

CHAPTER THIRTEEN
Christianese – A Religion in Bumper Stickers

The year was 1985, and Eastwood Church had no preacher. The previous pastor, Bill Hogue, had just taken a new job at the Southern Baptist Convention, and Eastwood was left to audition a replacement. I call it an audition because, despite all the platitudes about God's will, it was a panel of deacons—not God—who ultimately made the decision.

Enter Ruffin Snow, a beloved and wonderful man who came to Eastwood "in view of a call." In churchspeak, this meant he was applying for the pastor gig. Snow gave a guest sermon designed to impress the brain trust, and he was promptly hired. His appointment was declared divine providence.

I could never get my head around "in view of a call." I recently Googled the phrase, but no definition popped up. I know that Christians often speak of receiving a calling, a direct and unmistakable command from God to take up a task, job, or mission. So, Pastor Snow was looking for that calling? Or he was coming to see—or "view"—if Eastwood was his calling? Or he had arrived already knowing God's will and wanted the deacons to view the call? It has been almost four decades since that event, and I am no closer to understanding this little piece of Christianese.

When I say "Christianese," I am referring to informal, homogenous, and often vacant lingo intended to sound theologically profound. "God just laid it on my heart." "Our pastor really brings the Word." "The Bible helps us 'do life' together"—that kind of thing. Christianese simplifies the complex, complicates the simple, leans heavily into bumper-stickerisms, and often has the effect of making the speaker sound like they learned English from church marquees. In Christianese, you don't merely read the Bible, you "spend time in the Word." You aren't disconnecting from God, you are "backsliding." You aren't sharing time and food with friends, you are "fellowshipping." Your donation isn't a gift or tithe, it is a "love offering." You don't have a devotional, you have "quiet time."

I totally understand the appeal of tribal buzzwords. Every in-group winks its one-liners without apology. Yet Christianese is so saccharine, so caricaturized, and so unavoidable in the United States that it deserves special attention. (I am also inclined to write about it because, well, I just feel led.)

Catchy slogans dominate the modern church landscape, especially when it comes to branding. Church charities enjoy names like The Good Samaritans, Dare to Care, and Compassion Crew. Discipleship programs are sold as Walk Worthy or Rise & Shine. Missionaries become Harvesters, LifeGuards, or Wildfire. When I was growing up, I attended children's church and youth group. Today, parents can shuffle their kids off to Impact, Encounter, Oasis, ReGeneration, KidVenture, Fusion, Collision, One-Eighty, Xtreme Team, Basecamp, LIFT, Frontline, Aftershock, Elevate, and about a hundred other flavors of hip children's ministries modeled like mini-Disneylands. The messages are almost universal. Spread the Sonlight! Let go and let God!

Faith is bigger than fear! God is your co-pilot! Go get a faith-lift! It's not a religion, it's a relationship! He is risen! Honk if you love Jesus! This stuff is so sticky-sweet you could serve it with pancakes.

Christianese spills far into mainstream human expression. Insurance forms refer to an unforeseen or unpreventable natural disaster as an "act of God." People emerging from difficult circumstances speak of a "baptism by fire." Public figures enveloped in scandal have "fallen from grace." An uncertain or transitioning person is "in limbo." Self-righteous people are "holier than thou." Fact claims are deemed the "gospel truth."

But as we have already seen, Christianity engages a dictionary of vacuous lingo that is often reductive, shallow, or just jaw-droppingly stupid. And lest you think I am being unnecessarily harsh, remember that I spent decades parroting those same phrases as a believer. A personal favorite? "Bless your heart."

As this illustration demonstrates, "bless your heart" is a multi-tool that can serve a variety of purposes. It can build up, tear down, encourage, insult, praise, malign, engage, or dismiss. It has so many meanings that it risks having no meanings at all. Cases in point:

- A friend is diagnosed with the flu. "Bless your heart" is a show of sympathy.

- You bump into an old schoolmate at the mall. "Bless your heart" is a term of endearment.

- A friend shares anecdotes about his mission trip. "Bless your heart" shows support of the cause.

- You contradict someone's claim that geology proves Noah's flood. Their response of "bless your heart" is straight-up condescension as the Christian discredits you with pious love language. You poor thing; how misguided you are in your heart. (I have heard it said that inside every "bless your heart" there is a teeny tiny "fuck you.")

We see other phrases easily weaponized as well. "I'll pray for you" can be a wonderfully kind expression when a believer realizes you are in pain or experiencing difficulties. Remember that many Christians strongly believe that prayer is the first and best response to trouble, and their offerings of prayers on your behalf are simply an extension of that conviction. They aren't being dismissive. They are genuinely concerned and want to help.

Of course, we know how easily "I'll pray for you" can transform from empathy to disdain. Once, when I dared to inform a Christian that the Book of Genesis was not, in fact, written by Moses and that Moses may have never existed, they physically walked away, sneering the parting words, "I'll pray for you." On many occasions, believers smirk as they might at a child asking why God killed the dinosaurs. The phrase is a conversation stopper deployed from a high mountain of superiority. "You poor, sad little man. How deluded you are. I will talk to God about you."

If I may, I feel compelled to address the uncomfortable reality that "I'll pray for you" can also be a golden excuse for laziness. It is much easier to whisper a prayer than to deliver meals to a shut-in or take over the household chores of a cancer patient. Empty words of concern are easier than giving money to people who can't pay their electric bill or fix the old pickup they drive to work. "I'll pray for you" then becomes a "Get Out of Helping Free" card. As the saying goes:

To be fair, many Christians engage in acts of service while supplementing their charity with prayers because they embrace the words of James 2:17: "Faith without works is dead." In this context, "I'll pray for you" isn't a dig or an excuse to check out. The believer is simply and sincerely trying to stack the deck in your favor.

Ultimately, as with so many expressions, it all comes down to intent, but the next time someone says, "I'll pray for you," notice how the sentence is used. Is it a kind expression of concern, a substitute for tangible help, or a slap in the face?

Another reproach-disguised-as-kindness Christian platitude is, "I say this in love." If you hear this one, set your jaw and wait for the round-house punch. (This one reminds me of how people use "with all due respect" just before saying you are full of crap.)

When I was a Christian, I had the lingo down. I spoke of being "intentional." I worked with churches that were "seeker-friendly" as I was "on the journey." Pastors encouraged me to "let go and let God." I wanted to "bear fruit" because I felt "a check in my spirit." Friends in my "life group" or "accountability group" would "pray a hedge of protection" around me, although some of those prayers were "unspoken." It was critical that I not be "worldly" but instead "set apart," so they would ask me, "How's your heart?" I would respond that I had been "struggling with my witness," but when I recommitted to Christ and "felt the spirit move," it was a "total God thing."

Secular people must find Christian mealtimes bizarre, as every breakfast, lunch, and dinner is preceded with a blessing. Family, friends, and associates gather around the table, an individual is appointed to lead the prayer, and divine magic is called down upon the chicken and mashed potatoes. "Oh Lord, please bless this food, nourish it to our bodies, and our bodies to your service. Amen."

On the surface, the act of praying seems like a generous and laudable thing. We stop. We reflect. We humbly bow our heads. We join to give thanks. If we don't scratch past the surface, prayer seems like a sensible and beautiful gesture beyond reproach. After all, who could ever criticize an act of looking beyond oneself to give thanks?

Let's focus for a moment on the potatoes. Recipes vary, but we can determine the basics: spuds, butter, whipping cream, salt, pepper, maybe some garlic and chives if we are feeling fancy. The table is set. The mashed goodness is hot and ready. Everyone gathers. The potatoes are blessed. Yet how is a blessed potato any different than the unblessed one? What physical change happens? Does the calorie count go down? Saturated fat? Cholesterol? Sodium? Do the vitamin ratios change? Is there a divine glow above the casserole dish? Do the potatoes give an energy boost or have healing properties?

The faithful are already dismissing questions I consider perfectly reasonable. If a prayer blesses food, has the edible become supernaturally supplemented in some way? Aren't Christians asking God to magically enchant a meal? And if this happens, why don't its physical properties change?

Some will argue that mealtime prayers are simply offerings of gratitude to God, blessings sent upward to the Father. Perhaps this makes sense, but phrasing the prayer as a blessing seems odd, especially against the fact that many of the blessers totally ignore the human hands that planted, cultivated, harvested, shipped, sold, and prepared the food that the Lord is being thanked for.

While traveling to these family festivities, the believer may pray for something called "traveling mercies." (My best translation for this prayer is, "Please, God, keep my car from getting T-boned at the four-way stop.") Ironically, those same Christians who name and claim God's "hedge of protection" hop into a vehicle equipped with scientifically developed safety features such as:

- seat belts
- front and side airbags

- perimeter and dash cameras
- impact-reduction bumpers
- child seat anchor systems
- anti-lock brakes with traction control
- lane-assist, collision prevention, and blind spot sensors

Why are the faithful paying extra for safety options not required by law? After all, God is the ultimate airbag!

Of course, we already know the answer. According to the National Safety Council, there are more than six million car collisions every year in the United States. Those collisions result in 4.4 million sustained injuries and more than thirty-eight thousand fatalities.[139] Given that roughly 65 percent of Americans identify as Christians,[140] we are looking at the statistical probability that 2.8 million of the injured and twenty-five thousand of the dead are Christians. Prayers for traveling mercies are obviously not protecting the faithful from calamity on American roads.

Yet the Bible promises God cares enough to count the hairs on their heads,[141] guaranteeing that "The Lord will keep you from all harm— he will watch over your life; the Lord will watch over your coming and going both now and forevermore."[142] Prayers for protection should result in (wait for it) *actual protection* per God's promise, "And I will do whatever you ask in my name, so that the Father may be glorified in the Son."[143] Sadly, pleas and petitions for traveling mercies seem to vanish into the ether. Maybe God is simply too busy making heavenly sunsets, or perhaps he wants or needs car accidents as part of his divine and perfect plan. As Christianese declares, everything happens for a reason.

I get why pattern-seeking primates constantly want to connect events to a higher purpose or destiny. Fortuitous events seem even more so when drawn in the frame of destiny. Walk into a Walmart a hundred times and you don't see anyone you know, but it only takes a single chance encounter with an old friend to trigger notions of divine providence. In the minds of many, there are no coincidences.

Interestingly, many Christians are keen on the ancient notions of karma, a spiritual principle of cause and effect. With karma, good intent and actions result in reciprocal goodness, and terrible intent and actions will visit future calamity upon you. It is a noble notion—and complete crap. As the internet meme says:

> # Dear Karma,
> # I know some people
> # that you missed.

Indeed, we can all think of people who spent decades cheating and abusing their fellow human beings without consequences, and we can also think of wonderful people who couldn't catch a break, spending the whole of their lives getting kicked in the teeth personally, relationally, financially, or physically. What kind of karma allows horrible agents to get away with it? What good reason would allow grifters to bankrupt their victims, violent parents to harm their children, murderous dictators to commit genocide?

Sadly, in light of the planet's pain and suffering, many believers shrug and say *que sera sera*, whatever will be will be. Even worse, many remain convinced that earthly suffering is a required precursor to Christ's return; pain in this life, bliss in the next. A church roof collapses on worshippers in Nigeria, killing sixty people? Everything happens for a reason. A ten-year-old boy is decapitated in a Kansas City water slide accident? Everything happens for a reason. Three hundred reindeer are killed by a lightning strike in Norway? Everything happens for a reason. In Christianity, this rationalization can easily be tied to this biblical promise: "And we know that in all things God works for the good of those who love him, who have been called according to his purpose."[144]

Cue the internet meme-verse, which eagerly affirms this notion with saccharine, fortune-cookie inanities so sweet that it is difficult to read them without insulin flooding your bloodstream. They also contradict each other at every turn.

Perfectly clear! God closes doors and opens other doors. Unless all doors remain closed in favor of a window exit. Unless all exits need to be closed. Unless Christ stands at the door and knocks. Unless Christ is already in the room as the Devil knocks. Or whatever. I am reminded of that clever line, "When God closes a door, open it. That's how doors work!"

Comedian and satirist Betty Bowers shared this clever meme, which correctly exposes the consequences for leaving Jesus on the porch.

Christians love their door metaphors. They also love water analogies. Indeed, it is not uncommon to see a billboard inviting everyone to *Living Water* Church, where the spirit *flows*, *washing* everyone in a *river* of peace and a *fountain* of joy, *raining* down God's blessings and bringing *waves* of glory back upon the Father. (OK, I am being facetious, but you get my drift.) Water metaphors ooze from Christian radio stations, church hymnals, and Sunday sermon notes.

For Olympic gold vacuousness, almost nothing competes with the phenomenon of church marquees, those ubiquitous signboards perched outside thousands of sanctuary doors. Passersby are treated to (ostensibly) profound Christianese gems such as these:

- Try praying instead of texting.
- Faith is like a rubber band; it must be stretched.
- Feeling puzzled? God is your missing peace. (Yes, they spell it that way.)
- Swallowing your pride won't give you indigestion.
- Be an organ donor; give your heart to Jesus!

As the COVID-19 pandemic raged, one marquee proclaimed, "Don't worry about the Delta! We have the Alpha & the Omega!" Hopefully, their hedge of protection included the COVID vaccine.

Of course, Christians aren't above their hell threats. Christian Aid Ministries has posted giant billboards in all fifty states with large-font messages such as, "Where are you going? Heaven or Hell?" The font for *Hell* is painted in orange flames. CAD anchors the signs with its handy toll-free number so that drivers can get instant redemption on the interstate. (Would that activate traveling mercies?)

One of my favorite examples of clumsy Christian wordplay is the (quickly deleted) 2013 tweet by Dallas megapastor Joel Osteen, which I post here with a base-level snicker:[145]

"Walk by faith" is another catchy line. The full verse commands

Joel Osteen ✔
@JoelOsteen

 Follow

A true friend walks in when everybody else walks out. A true friend doesn't rub it in when you make a mistake. They rub it out.

← Reply ⟲ Retweet ☆ Favorite ••• More

2,238
RETWEETS

1,227
FAVORITES

4:25 PM - 31 Oct 13

believers, "For we walk by faith, not by sight,"[146] a popular Christian morsel devoid of calories. Rephrased, the verse could say, "We believe things we cannot demonstrate or prove," or "We claim to know what we do not know." As Christopher Hitchens revealed, "It's called faith because it's not knowledge."

Every election season, you and I are forced to endure those syrupy political commercials for city, state, and federal candidates, with flags flying in the background as the narration assures us that that the candidate is a man of faith. Imagine that statement rewritten as it should be: "He is a man who claims to know what he does not know." This doesn't sound quite so impressive. In fact, I would wager that such an updated advertisement would send voters running toward the other candidate's booth.

Of course, believers protest that "I know it in my heart," which is a claim they would reject coming from an Islamist or a Hindu. Other religions are expected to bring facts and back up their Truth; Christianity gets to squeak by on faith. It is a huge double standard. As

Mark Twain famously said, "The easy confidence with which I know another man's religion is folly teaches me to suspect that my own is also."[147]

But wait! Believers challenged on this point will often pinball to evidence that Christianity is accurate and undeniable: complexity, beauty, prophecy, and so on. These Christians are then no longer walking by faith, which means they have just scratched out their beloved verse about doing so. Also, their evidence is easily debunked against the science. They might as well wear T-shirts reading, "God exists because I don't understand things."

The great philosopher Bertrand Russell summed up the problem in his famous quote, "Where there is evidence, no one speaks of faith. We do not speak of faith that two and two are four, or that the earth is round. We only speak of faith when we wish to substitute emotion for evidence."[148]

I have wandered a bit in this chapter, but whether we are talking about reductive fortune-cookie catchphrases or nonsensical apologetics applause lines, American Christianity loves its snappy mottos. Christianese reinforces in-group camaraderie, glosses over textured issues, projects religious chicness, and keeps Christian retailers busy printing T-shirts and window decals. It has also slipped so far into caricature that even fellow Christians mock it on the internet.

In fact, there seems to be a growing number of Christians who not only reject the half-baked catchphrases of Christianese but are purposefully distancing themselves from the God of the Bible to fashion a kinder, better, custom-fitted religion that embraces love and acceptance over oppression, sorcery, and cruelty. As we will see in the next chapter, these believers may declare themselves fundamental Christians, but the religion they practice is something else entirely.

CHAPTER FOURTEEN

Cherry Picking – The Custom-Fitting of Cafeteria Christianity

In this chapter, instead of discussing things that make Christians look and sound like idiots, I want to reverse gears and give twenty-first-century believers some credit for the idiotic things they are *not* doing. In other words, I want to compliment them for not adhering to the Bible. Like diners browsing the restaurant buffet for the most palatable offerings while rejecting the distasteful or disgusting, the cafeteria Christian selectively fills his or her spiritual plate with only the most appetizing fare.

Granted, it is quite possible that Christians omit some of God's stranger rules simply because they are unaware the rules exist. As I mentioned previously, the United States is a culture of Bible illiteracy, where Americans who can name all seven ingredients in a McDonald's Big Mac can't recite even half of the Ten Commandments.[149] Still, I would wager that most contemporary Christians blow off the Bible's prohibition on "a garment of cloth made of two kinds of material";[150] Christians love their polyester blends. Why would the omnipotent creator of a trillion planets care if cottons mixed with linens? I have no idea. But it is a stupid rule on a mountain of stupid rules, and Christians are usually smart enough to ignore it.

In the New Testament, men are commanded to keep the haircut tight: "Does not even nature teach you that it is a shame for a man to have long hair?"[151] Cue a conference of cool, hip pastors with shoulder-length locks, many looking not unlike the white Jesus paintings in their church vestibules. (Has anyone seen a depiction of Christ with *short* hair? Is the male God violating his own rule?)

Of course, this command contradicts various Old Testament scenarios in which "no razor shall touch his head,"[152] but remember that this is the same God who told Samuel, "Do not look on his appearance or on the height of his stature, because I have rejected him. For the Lord sees not as man sees; man looks on the outward appearance, but the Lord looks on the heart."[153]

So, God is saying that appearances both do and do not matter. Thanks, Yahweh. Of course, the Old Testament god is obsessed with physical appearances, so much so that he made a list of physical deformities that would disqualify priests from entering his temple:

> And the Lord spoke to Moses, saying, "Speak to Aaron, saying, 'None of your offspring throughout their generations who has a blemish may approach to offer the bread of his God. For no one who has a blemish shall draw near, a man blind or lame, or one who has a mutilated face or a limb too long, or a man who has an injured foot or an injured hand, or a hunchback or a dwarf, or a man with a defect in his sight or an itching disease or scabs or crushed testicles.'"[154]

Yes, God wants nobody on his holy doorstep who wouldn't qualify for the cover of *People* magazine because—let's face it—he is a shallow, petty, ableist asshole. Fortunately, his children (and often, his churches) are much more accommodating, accepting, and loving toward those with physical ailments and disabilities. Yahweh wasn't interested in wheelchair ramps, Braille signposts, sign language interpreters, and special-needs ministries for his tabernacle, but many Christians are, and they deserve appreciation for caring about people.

God created shellfish, then declared them an "abomination." In Leviticus he issues a prohibition on lobster, shrimp, and so on, because they are "detestable to you."[155] So, are believers skipping Sunday brunch at Red Lobster? Nope. Either they don't realize those verses exist in the Old Testament, they have dismissed them as obsolete (as if they ever made sense), or they just don't care.

Interestingly, many of these same old-covenant believers who reject the prohibition on shrimp embrace other Old Testament rules as law, including the Ten Commandments, the condemnation of non-heterosexuals, the marginalization of women, the whipping of children, and whatever else conveniently fits into their established opinions.

Still, Christians deserve credit for consuming crab, Leviticus be damned. In fact, that same Bible book lists a smorgasbord of banned foods that believers eat anyway: bacon, fish without fins or scales, deer, and even cows (which makes the American cheeseburger an abomination before God). Interestingly, God forbids the eating of "all flying insects that walk on all fours"[156] because he apparently forgot that insects have six legs, not four. Omniscience evidently has its limits.

Tattoos? Oh yes, they are taboo as well: "Do not cut your bodies for the dead or put tattoo marks on yourselves. I am the Lord."[157] Contemporary Christians not only ignore this prohibition, but they have embraced an entire industry of tattooed symbols representing their faith in Jesus: crosses, scriptures, thorns of the crucifixion, angels, and much more. The "body is a temple,"[158] yet believers are happy to decorate that temple as Yahweh grumbles from the tattoo parlor parking lot.

The New Testament tells women not to wear "elaborate hairstyles or gold or pearls or expensive clothes   ."[159] Tell that to the name-it-and-claim-it believers who drop more coin for a stylist and hand-bag than they will ever put in an offering plate. Christian couture is a thing. Just ask the prosperity gospel types and their silk-suited, diamond-studded megapastors.

As the fourth Commandment says, "Remember the Sabbath Day to keep it holy," so the seventh day of the week is considered sacred. God even executed a man for picking up twigs on a Saturday.[160] Against that directive, Christians are serial offenders. Their Sabbath days are loaded with activities. Some clock in at their jobs. Others clean house, or renovate, or work in the garden, or help friends with projects, or do any number of things that easily qualify as work. Unconcerned about breaking God's law, these Christians are simply living life and accomplishing tasks on their own terms, and that is a good thing.

Sex? Despite the strict model for a literally unadulterated biblical marriage, half of US Christians say that casual sex between adults is sometimes or always acceptable. (Six in ten Catholics agree.)[161] Masturbation? As we have discussed, Christians may huff and blush on the outside, but their numbers are included in the National Survey of Sexual Health and Behavior, which reveals that 78 percent of all Americans aged fourteen and older say they have self-pleasured at some point.[162] This rejection of puritanism isn't a bad thing, despite the warnings to have "self control," the command to "flee from sexual immorality," and the alarms about "the lust of the flesh."[163] Sexual expression is perfectly natural, and when believers embrace it, they are liberating both their bodies and their minds.

How many Christian relationships end in divorce? Pew Research puts the number at 51 percent among protestant believers—more than half! Yet the Bible declares that sexual immorality (an affair) is the only legitimate reason for a man to divorce his wife, and "anyone who marries a divorced woman commits adultery."[164] Do modern Christians avoid divorce when a marriage goes bad because they are worried about displeasing God? Certainly some do, but the statistics reveal that millions of the faithful cut marital cords and start fresh on their own terms—and good for them.

Relationships are complicated and often messy. Some deal-breaking issues aren't discovered until after the courthouse documents are signed, or, perhaps more often, people simply change, as do their attitudes, values, desires, and needs. I was a relative minnow when I first married at twenty-two. When I divorced almost two decades later, I had become a much different person. The Bible doesn't allow for change in this way. In fact, the Bible doesn't allow for much when it comes to the needs of the human heart. Marriage contracts are binding, even at the expense of decades of happiness, security, and safety.

Are Christian women mute in the churches? This is commanded in the New Testament: "As in all the congregations of the saints, women should remain silent in the churches," and yet we find thousands of female ministers in mainstream Christianity. Further, "I do not permit a woman to teach or assume authority over a man; she must be quiet,"[165] yet Christian women stomp on this command every single day as they speak, teach, and preach against misogyny. Granted, they are serving the God of misogyny as they rationalize his words, but I would rather have egalitarian, cafeteria Christianity than the fundie faith that silences half of the population.

We are plainly told, "Do not practice homosexuality, having sex with another man as with a woman. It is a detestable sin."[166] The book of Romans blasts women and men who do "shameful things" with each other.[167] Yet American Christianity is, more and more, making a place for non-heterosexuals in their auditoriums and even in some of their ministries. Granted, hardline Southern Baptists and other fundamentalist denominations are still in the dark ages on this issue, but those institutions are struggling against the increasingly progressive attitudes of believers more interested in acceptance than judgment. I am not speaking about the insidious conversion-therapy models for Christians and gay people, but rather a rising distaste for bigotry within congregations. Yahweh may have executed homosexuals, but many believers are committed to their protection, and good for them.

How many Christians have decided that spanking and whipping children does more harm than good? Yet parents are commanded to beat their children because "whoever spares the rod hates their children, but the one who loves their children is careful to discipline them."[168] The Bible loves its "smite" verses, and yet corporal punishment is decreasing in the United States. The General Social Survey, conducted by the nonpartisan and objective research organization NORC at the University of Chicago, measured a slow decline among born-again Christians who spank their kids. Corporal punishment dropped from 90 percent to under 80 percent, which is at least a move in the right direction. The American Psychological Association published an article on research showing that "spanking and other forms of physical discipline can pose serious risks to children."[169] Apparently, even some in the spare-the-rod crowd are beginning to heed those warnings. Discipline and physical beatings aren't the same thing, and Christians are evolving away from the commanded parental violence.

Christians cherish the Thirteenth Amendment to the US Constitution (declaring the abolition of slavery in the United States) while discarding the biblical instructions for the lawful owning and beating of slaves.[170] Some rationalize biblical slavery as indentured servitude (a fallacy), and others uncomfortably blink it away. Regardless, Christians are resisting the bigotry of their own Bibles. They reject the idea that one person may own another as property, and this is a good and necessary thing.

Psychologist Valerie Tarico penned an article on Bible verses Christians love to ignore, diving into how "some Bible-believing Christians play fast and loose with their sacred text."[171] Some commands are strange and culty, such as the rules for ox slaughter and making round haircuts. Some are just weird and pointless, such as don't eat owls. Others are straight-up offensive: "unclean" menstruating women are to be banned from their towns for seven days.

Meanwhile, today's Christianity comprises mostly Bible-illiterate communities spoon-fed on Sundays while living secular lives every other day of the week. Their faith is meaningful in terms of community and comfort, but it is irrelevant to many of their day-to-day decisions about the things that matter. Their religion goes no further than the Jesus fish decal on the car window, the dusty Bible on the nightstand, the catchy Hillsong tune on the radio, and the painted scripture sign above the doorway of their home. They don't know where the books of the Bible came from. They are ignorant of Jesus studies and comparative analyses of the Gospels. They are unaware of Revelation's apocalypse narratives beyond bumper stickers about Heaven and Hell. They live in a warm and happy cocoon of belief in belief.

Sure, religious bigotry and fearmongering remains a huge problem, but in the United States at least, we are slowly seeing Christianity's evolution into a "faith lite" model. ("I believe in Jesus, but I'm not religious"; that kind of thing.) Christians uninterested in judgment and hellfire are leaving the pews and discarding ugly doctrines, and I think this is a necessary, positive trend. I hope it will ultimately lead to some hard and critical analysis of the entire Christian religion. As the saying goes, If you have to distance yourself from fundamentalism, there is something wrong with your religion's fundamentals.

I think the religious rejection of destructive dogma speaks to innate human goodness, and it often requires real courage and integrity to reject religious party lines. Cafeteria Christianity reveals a yearning for better ideas and ideals by thoughtful, generally reasonable people. At the very least, in the arena of ideas, they often cull the nonsensical and the outright immoral. For this, they have my admiration and appreciation.

As I said in the introduction, I am not implying that Christians themselves are idiots any more than human beings in general are idiots. I wasn't stupid during my thirty years as an evangelical Christian, nor did my IQ spike when I left religion in 2008. I had the same brain operating at the same tempo as I have now. This is a point I constantly make when atheists accuse God believers of being as dull as dryer lint. Christians are often smart, sharp people who deserve to be treated with respect and grace. Their lives are loaded with goodness, care, empathy, charity, joy, and the genuine desire to do what is right. Many of the best people in my life are Christians, and I cherish them dearly. They are not caricatures. They are not brainless twits. They live good lives, love their children, help others in need, and pursue worthy goals and dreams with every desire to do the right things. I cannot stress this enough.

But I will say with absolute conviction that *Christianity itself is idiocy*. The whole religion is the product of primitive times and ignorant minds. Its sacred texts speak of wizards and blood magic, of talking donkeys and towering giants, of nine-hundred-year-old humans and people living underwater in the bellies of fish. Christianity has enslaved and oppressed. Its god slaughtered countless men, women, babies, villages, towns, cities, whole cultures. It silences women and discriminates against every flavor of out-group. At its core, it is a fear cult shouting "Jesus loves you!" against the threat of eternal torment. It is nonsense. It is offensive. It is stupid. And for two thousand years, it has made believers spew nonsense designed to sound profound.

What would be genuinely profound? To slough off the bonds of ancient superstitions, to plant our feet in the real world, to measure our words and deeds against good data and good sense, and to constantly ask ourselves if we are speaking and acting in meaningful, inclusive, critical, constructive, and enlightened ways. In my opinion, that approach is the best way to idiot-proof ourselves in this crazy world.

CHAPTER FIFTEEN
Reflection – Pointing the Finger Back at Myself

Matthew 7:3 famously asks the question, "Why do you look at the speck of sawdust in your brother's eye and pay no attention to the plank in your own eye?" Pardon my irony as I lean in to that verse's larger point about introspection. I have spent much of my career as an atheist activist gawking and pointing at the bizarre, nonsensical, and offensive traits of my former faith, but my indictments still strike extremely close to home; as I criticize Christianity, I am also criticizing the younger version of myself. For decades, I was a gear in the Christian machine, guilty of bad reasoning (or no reasoning) as I danced to my family's religious tune.

I was doubtful of an easterly Rapture at my grandmother's funeral, but I still embraced the belief that the skies would soon split wide as the Messiah returned. I didn't buy into the worry that burials should be directional, but I was convinced that the dead would arise from their graves for a divine reunion in the clouds. It is interesting that I could be so skeptical about that single aspect of the Second Coming while eagerly—and blindly—embracing the biblical claim of a holy zombie emergence.

I took communion and enjoyed it. The practice had been baked into my consciousness so deeply that it would have felt abnormal *not* to partake. Beginning in early childhood I was steeped in the violent imagery of the crucified Christ, and I proudly proclaimed myself washed in the blood, covered by the blood, redeemed through the blood. Of course, before any blood could cleanse me, it first had to be spilled, and I spent decades believing that the stark Bible tales of hammers, spikes, whips, thorns, crosses, and graves were perfectly reasonable stories to tell other people—especially children.

I whispered my prayers for everyday things. I asked God for blessings upon my chicken dinner, to find my lost car keys, to get rid of a headache; I was eager to celebrate divine intervention whenever fortune turned in my favor. I thanked God for the groceries bought with my weekly paychecks. I credited God for the successful surgeries performed by trained, expert physicians. I thanked God for the sun on clear days and for the rain on stormy ones. All the while, I was eager to give God credit whenever something went my way. (Misfortune was blamed on a sinful world, and often, the Devil directly.) My brain had lazily drifted into an acceptance of good luck and happy coincidences as divine favor. I might have easily credited Jesus for giving me the location of a lost bicycle while ignoring or excusing God's absence in the human struggles that really mattered.

I was both a chest-thumping moralist and a hypocrite, spouting outwardly the language of purity while wrestling with "impure" thoughts and desires. I harbored a hidden self beneath the piety, proudly protesting the natural world while simultaneously being a part of it. My biology textbooks were Bible workbooks. My history books were doctrinal statements. I sang about freedom from within prison walls. My understanding of my body, my person, and my world was distilled into Christian catchphrases and Bible verses. I custom-fitted almost every circumstance into the shape of divine providence. My thinking was simplistic. My mind was locked. My world was small.

It is interesting to examine my former religious self from the vantage point of a middle-aged skeptic not just because I am older (and hopefully wiser), but also because my introduction to new people, fresh ideas, and better information liberated me from within and without. I will always wince at the memory of the young Seth Andrews clucking his Christianese, but I will also feel gratitude that those decades gave me an insider's perspective on the religious cultures that so often produce the strangest of thoughts and behaviors.

I can be hard on Christianity (and my younger Christian self), but I haven't lost my empathy for people. I have found the ability to distinguish between smart people and stupid behaviors because I once fit the model. In fact, I have come to learn how adept intelligent people can be at rationalizing the irrational, essentially outsmarting themselves into opinions and actions that make no logical sense. Human beings are complex, fascinating creatures that don't fit into a box, and this is true for the religious as well.

I have often said that people deserve respect in the general sense but that ideas must earn respect, and I stand by that assertion. There are no sacred cows. No notion, opinion, claim, practice, tradition, ideology, or theology is off limits. Put up or shut up; it is all fair game, especially in the context of the damage bad ideas can inflict. It stands to reason that faux executions, blood rituals, purity cults, and the distractions of magical thinking aren't serving to connect humanity to the real world, and the insular alternate reality of Christian culture often hamstrings the very people it claims to help.

I am not immune from sounding like an idiot—I am human, after all—but I am convinced that my departure from the religious bubble has helped me to develop a personal relationship with reality. In the real world, I have more and better opportunities to meet people where they are, accept them for who they are, learn about the world and the universe as they are, and can better focus my energies on the things that matter.

No ancient texts or supernatural dogma has ever brought me the satisfaction I feel now that I am outside religious walls, and it is my hope that others can find their footing and carve their own paths into a better, more curious, more thoughtful, more accepting, more reasonable, and more satisfying world.

Acknowledgments

Authors, producers, artists, and creators of all stripes don't exist in a bubble. At the very least, I don't. The whole of my work as a broadcaster, writer, speaker, and activist is made possible by wonderful people who move and motivate me.

Special thanks to my wife and love, Natalie, for her constant support. Thanks as well to Vincent Deporter for his illustrations, which took each chapter of this book to another level. My gratitude to Jessica Vineyard at Red Letter Editing for honing my thoughts and keeping me on track. My appreciation to Gayle Jordan for her generous foreword, as well as to her entire team at Recovering from Religion. And I can't express enough how honored I am to serve The Thinking Atheist community and podcast audience. They are my family all over the world, and they make each day, each project, each moment something unique and special.

Endnotes

1. John 14:15.
2. Joyce Meyer, *Battlefield of the Mind for Teens: Winning the Battle in Your Mind*, New York: Hatchet Book Group, 2006.
3. 2018 Pew Research Center's American Trends Panel, April 23-May 6, 2018. See also Cary Funk, Greg Smith, David Masci, "How Many Creationists Are There in America?," *Scientific American*, Feb. 12, 2019.
4. Melanie Challenger, *How to Be Animal: A New History of What It Means to Be Human*, New York: Penguin Books, 2021.
5. Patrick Yesudian, "Human Hair – An Evolutionary Relic?" *International Journal of Trichology*, vol. 3, issue 2, Jul-Dec 2011.
6. Robert Shmerling, MD, "Wondering About Goosebumps? Of Course You Are," Harvard Health Publishing, Oct. 2, 2020.
7. Laura Clark, "Before Agriculture, Human Jaws Were a Perfect Fit for Human Teeth," *Smithsonian Magazine*, Feb. 6, 2015.
8. "Why Do Most People Have Their Wisdom Teeth Pulled?," Corson Dentistry.
9. Kara Rogers, "7 Vestigial Features of the Human Body," Britannica.
10. "Vestigial Organs," Science Oxford, July 17, 2015.

11. Jesse Bering, "A Bushel of Facts about the Uniqueness of Human Pubic Hair," *Scientific American*, March 1, 2010.

12. Gen. 1:26.

13. Magdalia Campobasso & Jessica O'hara, "From Descartes to Goodall: Humans' Claims about Animal Intelligence," Penn State, Nov. 2017.

14. *The Philosophy of Animal Minds*, Robert Lurz (ed.), New York: Cambridge University Press, 2009.

15. Clifford Lazarus, PhD, "Why Many People Stubbornly Refuse to Change Their Minds," *Psychology Today*, Dec. 24, 2018.

16. Briony Swire-Thompson, Joseph DeGutis & David Lazera, "Searching for the Backfire Effect: Measurement and Design Considerations," *JARMAC*, vol. 9, issue 3, Sept. 2020.

17. Jonas T. Kaplan, Sarah I. Gimbel & Sam Harris, "Neural Correlates of Maintaining One's Political Beliefs in the Face of Counterevidence," *Scientific Reports* 6, Dec. 2016.

18. Kate Wong, "The 1 Percent Difference," *Scientific American*, Sept. 2014.

19. Anna Muir, "10 Ways Chimps and Humans are the Same," The Jane Goodall Institute of Canada.

20. Henry Mance, interview, "Frans de Waal: 'We Are Very Much Like Primates'" *Financial Times*, March 8, 2019. See also Frans de Waal, *Mama's Last Hug: Animal Emotions and What They Tell Us about Ourselves*, New York: W.W. Norton & Company, 2019.

21. Abby Hafer, *The Not-So-Intelligent Designer: Why Evolution Explains the Human Body and Intelligent Design Does Not*, Eugene, OR: Cascade Books, 2015.

22. Michael Ruse, "Intelligent Design Is an Oxymoron" *The Guardian*, May 5, 2010.

23. David Mikkelson, "666 Barcode," Snopes.com, April 27, 2011.

24. "Devout Christian Horrified Over 'Satanic' 666 License Plate from DMV," KPIX CBS SF Bay Area, April 24, 2015.

25. Elizabeth Dwoskin, "On Social Media, Vaccine Misinformation Mixes with Extreme Faith," *Washington Post*, Feb. 16, 2021.

26. Joseph Choi, "Marjorie Taylor Greene Blasts COVID-19 Vaccine Passports: 'Biden's Mark of the Beast,'" The Hill, March 30, 2021.

27. Linda Rodriguez McRobbie, "On the Science of Creepiness," *Smithsonian Magazine*, Oct. 29, 2015.

28. Joy Cunningham, *Witchcraft: Witchcraft for Beginners and Wicca Starter Kit*, independently published, 2019.

29. 2 Cor. 6:14.

30. "Billy Graham: Satan Is Real and Should be Feared," *The Kansas City Star*, July 1, 2016.

31. John Piper, "Satan's Ten Strategies Against You," desiringGod. org, Oct. 4, 2016.

32. Chuck Todd, Mark Murray & Carrie Dann, "Study Finds Nearly One-In-Five Americans Believe QAnon Conspiracy Theories," Meet the Press, NBC News, May 27, 2021.

33. Rev.17:17.

34. See Rev. 8:7; Rev. 8:10-11; Rev. 15-16; Rev. 17; Rev. 9:11; Rev. 12:1-2; Rev. 6:12-17; Rev. 19:1-21.

35. Eph. 6:10-11.

36. Matt. 5:10.

37. "Faith on the Hill: The Religious Composition of the 116th Congress," Pew Research Center, Jan. 3, 2019.

38. National Congregations Study, Mark Chaves (principal investigator), NORC & University of Chicago, 2020.

39. Ralph Waldo Emerson journal entry, Nov. 8, 1838.

40. Annie Waldman, "Study: Religious Children are Less Able to Distinguish Fantasy from Reality," BBC News, July 29, 2014.

41.   Rick Robin Cope, "Thank you Jesus for the Blood!," Facebook, April 4, 2021.

42.   E.A. Hoffman, "Are You Washed in the Blood?," music & lyrics, 1878.

43.   George Bennard, "The Old Rugged Cross," music & lyrics, 1912.

44.   CarlP, "I can't believe I used to sing about being washed in blood like it was totally normal," Twitter, March 27, 2021.

45.   Plutarch, *Moralia, Volume V: Isis and Osiris*, Loeb Classical Library Ed., 1936.

46.   Kenneth Grahame Rea, "The Abydos Passion Play," Western Theater, Ancient Egypt, Britannica.

47.   Osiris, Ancient Religions and Mythology, Britannica.

48.   Samuel Kramer, *History Begins at Sumer: Thirty-Nine Firsts in Recorded History*, 3rd ed., Pennsylvania: University of Pennsylvania Press, 1988.

49.   Plutarch, *Romulus*, 75 ACE.

50.   Herodotus, *The Histories Book II*, ch. 145, est. 426-415 BCE.

51.   Ps. 51:5; Rom. 7:14; Ps. 58:3; Rom. 3:9; Rev. 20:15; Matt. 13:42.

52.   Ira F. Stanphill, "Unworthy," music & lyrics.

53.   Matt. 26:26-27.

54.   Donald J. Wiseman, *Illustrations from Biblical Archaeology*, Carol Stream, Illinois: The Tyndale Press, 1958.

55.   See Matt. 26:20-25; Mark 14:17-21; John 13:21-30; see Luke 22:21-23; see Matt. 26:26-29; Mark 14:22-25; see Luke 22:17-20.

56.   Fr. William Saunders, "Transubstantiation," Catholic Education Resource Center, 2005.

57.   Becka A. Alper, "6 Facts about What Americans Know about Religion," Pew Research Center, July 23, 2019.

58.   Francis J. Ripley, "Transubstantiation for Beginners," Catholic

Answers, July 1, 1993.

59. "Transubstantiation," see n. 56.

60. United States Conference of Catholic Bishops, "The Real Presence of Jesus Christ in the Sacrament of the Eucharist: Basic Questions and Answers," June 2001.

61. Damien Marsic and Mehran Sam, "DNA Analysis of Consecrated Sacramental Bread Refutes Catholic Transubstantiation Claim," Scientific Raelian, Oct. 25, 2014.

62. The Vatican "Code of Canon Law."

63. Authorship is estimated between 70 and 150 CE. Along with the other consensus scholarship, see Bart Ehrman, "How Do We Know When the Gospels Were Written?," The Bart Ehrman Blog, Sept. 21, 2018.

64. Mitchell Reddish, *An Introduction to the Gospels*, Nashville, TN: Abingdon Press, 1997.

65. I Thess. 4:16.

66. 1 John 3:20; see Matt. 10:30; Heb. 4:13; Job 28:24.

67. Dimitris Xygalatas, "Why People Need Rituals, Especially in Times of Uncertainty," The Conversation, March 25, 2020.

68. John W. Loftus, *The Outsider Test for Faith: How to Know Which Religion Is True*, Amherst, NY: Prometheus Books, 2013.

69. Gal. 5:22-23.

70. See Ps. 137:9; Deut. 22:28-29; 2 Chron. 13:16.

71. "The Bible in America: 6-Year Trends," Barna, June 15, 2016.

72. Stephen Prothero, *Religious Literacy: What Every American Needs to Know—and Doesn't*, New York: HarperCollins, 2008.

73. Stephen Prothero, interviewed by Taylor McNeil, "Pray Tell: What Americans Don't Know About Religion," BU Today, Boston University, March 5, 2007.

74. Thomas Paine, *The Age of Reason*, Chicago: GE Wilson, 1893.

75.   "Science Inclusion Procedure," Answers in Genesis.

76.   Answers in Genesis, "Statement of Faith."

77.   Carl Sagan, *Broca's Brain: Reflections on the Romance of Science*, 3rd ed., New York: Random House, 1979.

78.   William Lane Craig, "The *Kalam* Cosmological Argument," Reasonable Faith, with William Lane Craig.

79.   Frank Turek, Twitter, Dec. 2021.

80.   Prov. 3:5.

81.   1 Cor. 1:27.

82.   James Dobson, *When God Doesn't Make Sense: Holding Onto Your Faith During the Hardest Times*, Carol Stream, Illinois: Tyndale House Publishers, 2012.

83.   Doug Powel, "The Use and Abuse of Christian Apologetics," Lifeway Research, Nov. 6, 2019.

84.   Isa. 45:15.

85.   1 Cor. 14:33.

86.   Heb. 4:13.

87.   Franklin Graham, "Did God lend a hand in freeing the Ever Given?" Facebook, March 31, 2021.

88.   Laura Ingraham, lauraingraham.com.

89.   Lance West, "'She's here with you,' Hidden miracle Bible found in tornado rubble," Oklahoma News 4, April 27, 2015.

90.   Maria Konnikova, "Why We Need Answers," *The New Yorker*, April 30, 2013.

91.   2 Cor. 4:17.

92.   Rom. 11:34.

93.   Bruce L. Newman, "Constitutional Law – The Problem with Obscenity," *Case Western Reserve Law Review*, vol. 11, issue 4, 1960.

94.   Cohen v. California, United States Supreme Court, 1971.

95.   Tala Esmaili, "Obscenity," Cornell Law School Legal Infor-

mation Institute. Last updated June 2017.

96. Bob Smietana, "Americans Worry About Moral Decline, Can't Agree on Right and Wrong," Lifeway Research, May 9, 2017.

97. "Hays Code," American Historama, Siteseen Limited, 2017.

98. "There are more than one billion firearms in the world, the vast majority of which are in civilian hands," Small Arms Survey, Geneva, Switzerland, June 2018.

99. WIN/Gallup 2014 End Of Year Survey.

100. "Quality of Life," *U.S. News & World Report*, 2021.

101. Anna Brown, "Nearly Half of U.S. Adults Say Dating Has Gotten Harder for Most People in the Last 10 Years," Pew Research Center, Aug. 20, 2020.

102. 2 Tim. 2:9; 1 Peter 3:33; Prov. 31:30.

103. Prov. 7:10; 2 Kings 9:30; Isaiah 3:16.

104. David M. Buss, *The Evolution of Desire: Strategies of Human Mating*, New York: Basic Books, 2016. First published in 1994.

105. "National Survey of Family Growth" 2016, and "National Longitudinal Survey of Adolescent to Adult Health" 2012, Centers for Disease Control and Prevention.

106. *Evolution*, see n. 104.

107. Kellie Jeppson, "Virtue Makes You Beautiful," YouTube.

108. Amanda Robb, "The Innocence Project," *O: The Oprah Magazine*, March 2007.

109. "Estimated Median Age of Americans at their First Wedding in the United States from 1998 to 2019, by Sex," Statista, Jan. 20, 2021.

110. Living Word Christian Center International Ministries, "True Love Waits" pledge.

111. See Gen. 2.

112. See Gen. 16:1.

113. *Ibid.*
114. Polygamists as identified in the Bible: Esau: Gen. 26; David: 2 Sam. 12; Solomon: 1 Kings 11; Belshazzar: Dan. 5.
115. See Deut. 22:28-29.
116. See Num. 31; Deut. 21.
117. 1 Cor. 7:10.
118. "Teen Birth Rate By State," National Center for Health Statistics, Centers for Disease Control and Prevention.
119. Benjamin Edelman, "Red Light States: Who Buys Online Adult Entertainment?," *Journal of Economic Perspectives* 23, no 1, winter, 2009.
120. "2017 Year In Review," PornHub Insights, Jan. 9, 2018.
121. "Share of American Women Who Have Ever Masturbated Alone in Their Lifetime as of 2009, by Age Group," Statista, 2021.
122. Matt. 10:28; 2 Tim. 1:7; Heb. 13:6.
123. Matt. 10:31.
124. Jon Niccum, "Religion Shapes American Attitudes About Gun Ownership, Study Shows," University of Kansas, Aug. 3, 2020. See also Abigail Vegter & Margaret Kelley, "The Protestant Ethic and the Spirit of Gun Ownership" *Journal for the Scientific Study of Religion*, vol 29, issue 3, Sept. 2020.
125. Matt. 24:36.
126. Nicole Spector, interview with David Spiegel, "This Is Your Brain on Prayer and Meditation," Better by Today, NBC News, Oct. 20, 2017.
127. E. Mohandas, "Neurobiology of Spirituality," *Mens Sana Monographs*, 6(1); Jan-Dec 2008.
128. Tanya Luhrmann, "Prayer Failure," *Psychology Today*, May 12, 2012.
129. 1 John 5:14-15.
130. See 2 Kings 5:9-10; Matt. 9:20-22; Mark 2:9-12; John 9:6-7;

John 11; Matt. 9:35.

131. See Matt. 21:22; John 14:13-14.

132. Anonymous, "Stop Cancer. Start Praying." Facebook, nd.

133. "Global Cancer Facts & Figures," American Cancer Society, 2018.

134. 2 Cor. 4:17.

135. Rom. 8:28.

136. See 1 John 1:8.

137. Herbert Benson, et al., "Study of the Therapeutic Effects of Intercessory Prayer in Cardiac Bypass Patients," *American Heart Journal*, April 2006, 151(4): 934-42.

138. Stanton Peele, "Public Prayers Do More Harm than Good," *Psychology Today*, Dec. 11, 2010.

139. "Car Crash Deaths and Rates," National Safety Council.

140. "In U.S., Decline of Christianity Continues at Rapid Pace," Pew Research Center, Oct. 17, 2019.

141. Matt. 10:30.

142. Ps. 121:7-8.

143. John 14:13.

144. Rom. 8:28.

145. Joel Osteen, "A true friend," Twitter, Oct. 31, 2013.

146. 2 Cor. 5:7.

147. Albert Bigelow, *Mark Twain: A Biography*, Sydney, Australia: Wentworth Press, 2016.

148. Bertrand Russell, *Human Society in Ethics and Politics*, New York: Routledge Classics ed., 2010. Originally published in 1954.

149. "Americans Know Big Macs Better than Ten Commandments" Reuters Life!, Reuters, Oct. 12, 2007.

150. Lev. 19.

151. 1 Cor. 11:14.

152. Judges 13:5; Num. 6:5.

153. 1 Sam. 16:7.

154. Lev. 21:16-20.

155. Lev. 11:9-12.

156. Lev. 11:20.

157. Lev. 19:28.

158. 1 Cor. 6:19.

159. 1 Tim. 2:9.

160. Num. 15.

161. Jeff Diamant, "Half of U.S. Christians say casual sex between consenting adults is sometimes or always acceptable," Pew Research Center, Aug. 31, 2020.

162. National Survey of Sexual Health and Behavior, Indiana University, Bloomington.

163. Gal. 5:22-23; 1 Cor. 6:18; 1 John 2:16.

164. Matt. 5:32.

165. 1 Cor. 14:34; 1 Tim. 2:12.

166. Lev. 18:22.

167. Rom. 1:18-32.

168. Prov. 13:24.

169. Brendan L. Smith, "The Case against Spanking," April 2012, vol. 43, no. 4.

170   Exod. 21.

171   Valerie Tarico, "11 Kinds of Bible Verses Christians Love to Ignore," AlterNet, May 26, 2014.

CPSIA information can be obtained
at www.ICGtesting.com
Printed in the USA
LVHW031041200322
713908LV00003B/368